NCERT PRACTICE WORK BOOK

MATHEMATICS

MATH-MAGIC

ARIHANT PRAKASHAN, MEERUT

WORKBOOK Mathematics 1st

Published by Arihant Prakashan, Meerut

Administrative & Production Offices

Regd. Office
'Ramchhaya' 4577/15, Agarwal Road, Darya Ganj, New Delhi -110002
Tele: 011- 47630600, 43518550; Fax: 011- 23280316

Head Office
Kalindi, TP Nagar, Meerut (UP) - 250002
Tel: 0121-2401479, 2512970, 4004199; Fax: 0121-2401648

Sales & Support Offices
Agra, Ahmedabad, Bengaluru, Bhubaneswar, Bareilly, Chennai, Delhi, Guwahati, Hyderabad, Jaipur, Jhansi, Kolkata, Lucknow, Meerut, Nagpur & Pune

ISBN 978-93-11122-09-0

Price ₹ 80.00

Production Team

Publishing Manager
Keshav Mohan, Amit Verma

Project Head
Karishma Yadav

Project Coordinator
Pooja Chaudhary

Project Editor
Priya Mittal

Cover Designer
Shanu Mansoori

DTP Operator
Ravi Sagar, Kamal Kishor

Figure Illustrator
Brahampal Singh

For further information about the books published by Arihant, log on to **www.arihantbooks.com** or e-mail at **info@arihantbooks.com**

Workbook, Why?

"Knowledge will not be with you for Long Unless You Practice"

This quotation answer the above question 'Workbook, Why?' perfectly, i.e. Workbooks are made to give the students practice required to achieve perfection & mastery in the subject. These are the only Workbooks, which are strictly based on **NCERT, the only recommended books by Govt. of India & CBSE** (reference Circular No. Acad-41/2015 dated 20th July 2015).

Given below is the detailed description of Workbook and some of its special features

ONLY WORKBOOK BASED ON NCERT

NCERT textbooks are the only textbooks, which have been prepared according to National Curriculum Framework, which discourages the idea of rote learning rather they focus on understanding and try to make the students able to identify the way of problem solving.

Keeping the importance of NCERT textbooks in mind we have prepared this Workbook, strictly based on NCERT content, this Workbook will complement NCERT by providing practice on the material given in each chapter of NCERT textbook, making the students understand the chapter completely.

WORKBOOK- PURPOSE, USE & FEATURES

This Workbook, through its **numerous exercises** having different **variety of questions** covering each and every fact of NCERT, will prove to be **equally useful** for both, **Classroom** and at **Home**. One more purpose of this Workbook is to provide the students a **systematic practice** of the content taught in the class and what they study in the textbooks.

Some special features of this workbook are

- Complete Coverage of each chapter for complete practice
- Different variety of questions; Fill in the Blanks, True-False, Matching, Multiple Choice Questions, Word Problems, etc.
- Many Questions given in each chapter are related with day-to-day activities making them interesting to solve.
- Keeps the students actively engaged with the content and develop enquiry skills.

WORKBOOK-DESIGNED TO IMPROVE SUBJECT ABILITIES

All the material given in this workbook is tailored to suit subject content with equal support on learning, which will surely help students to boost their abilities and confidence in the subject.

We look forward for the feedback from students, teachers and parents for the further improvement of the contents of this book. We will try to update the contents according to your feedback in further editions of this Workbook.

The Publisher

Contents

[Chapter **1**]

Shapes and Space

1 Tick (✓) the objects which are inside and cross (✗) the objects which are outside.

2 Colour the picture which is bigger.

(i)

(ii)

(iii)

(iv)

3 Look at the pictures below. Tick (✓) the pictures which are biggest and cross (✗) the pictures which are smallest in each part.

(i)

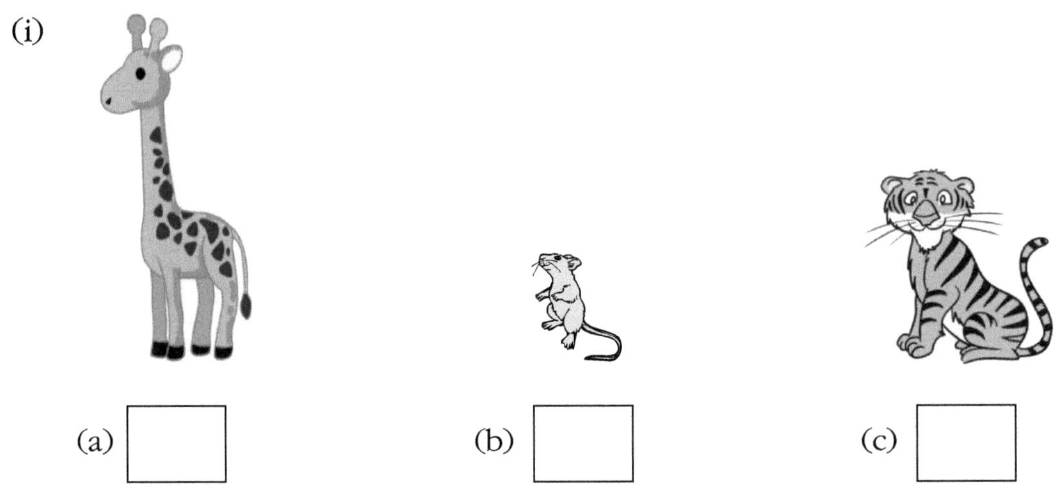

(a) ☐ (b) ☐ (c) ☐

(ii)

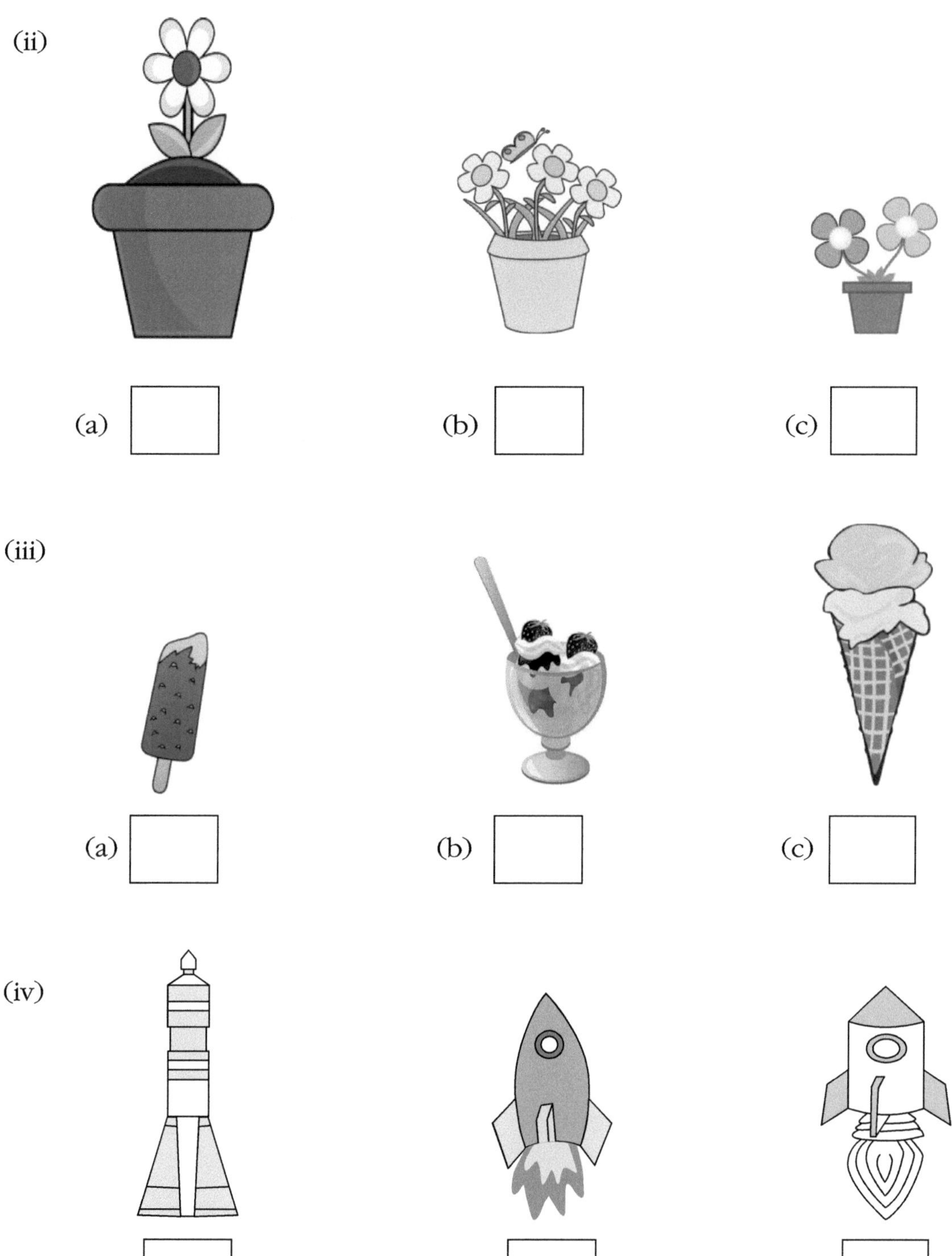

(a) ☐ (b) ☐ (c) ☐

(iii)

(a) ☐ (b) ☐ (c) ☐

(iv)

(a) ☐ (b) ☐ (c) ☐

4 (i) Tick (✓) the pot at the bottom.

(ii) Tick (✓) book on the top.

(iii) Tick (✓) flower on the top.

(iv) Tick (✓) rabbit at the bottom.

5 (i) Tick (✓) the tree which is nearer to the boy.

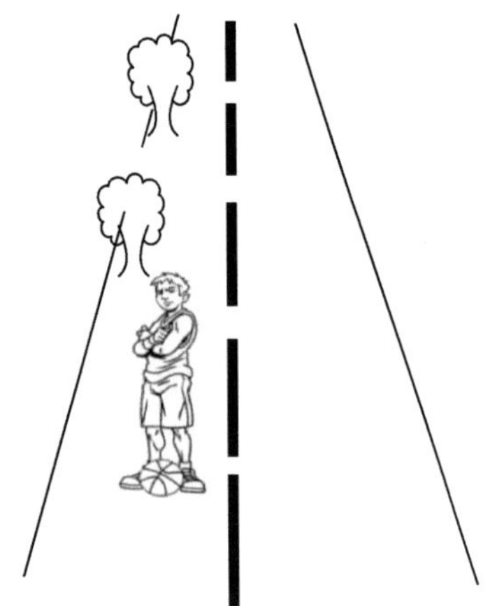

(ii) Tick (✓) the person who is farther from the bus.

(iii) Tick (✓) the car which is nearer to the traffic signal.

6 (i) Tick (✓) the cat which is nearest to the rat.

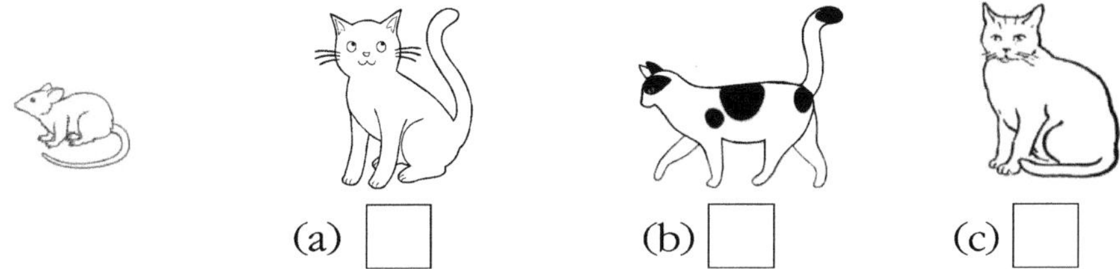

(a) ☐ (b) ☐ (c) ☐

(ii) Tick (✓) the car which is farthest from the boy.

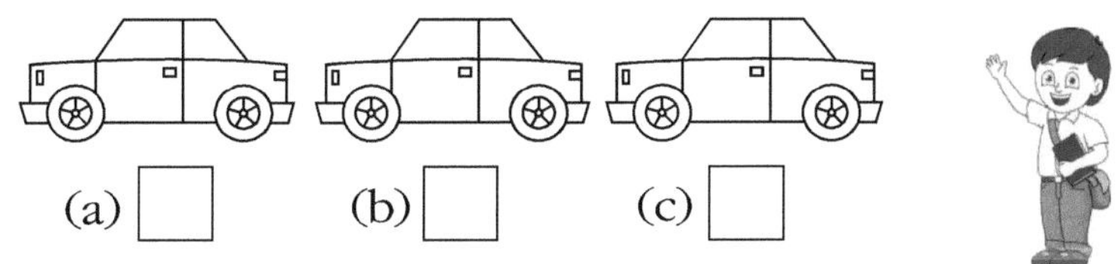

(a) ☐ (b) ☐ (c) ☐

(iii) Tick (✔) the child which is nearest to the bus.

(a) ☐ (b) ☐ (c) ☐

(iv) Tick (✔) the bird which is farthest from the tree.

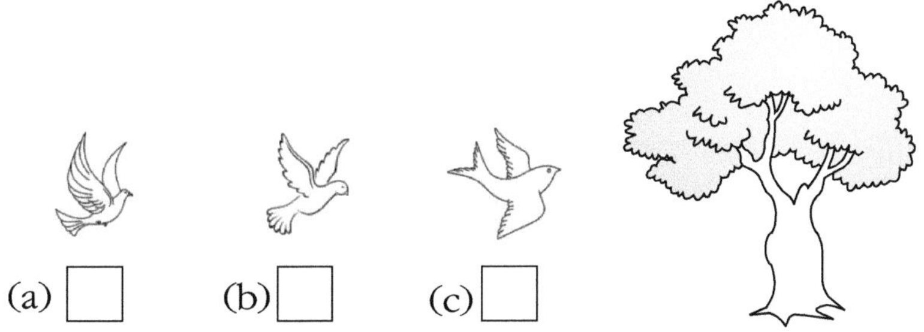

(a) ☐ (b) ☐ (c) ☐

7 Fill in the blanks.

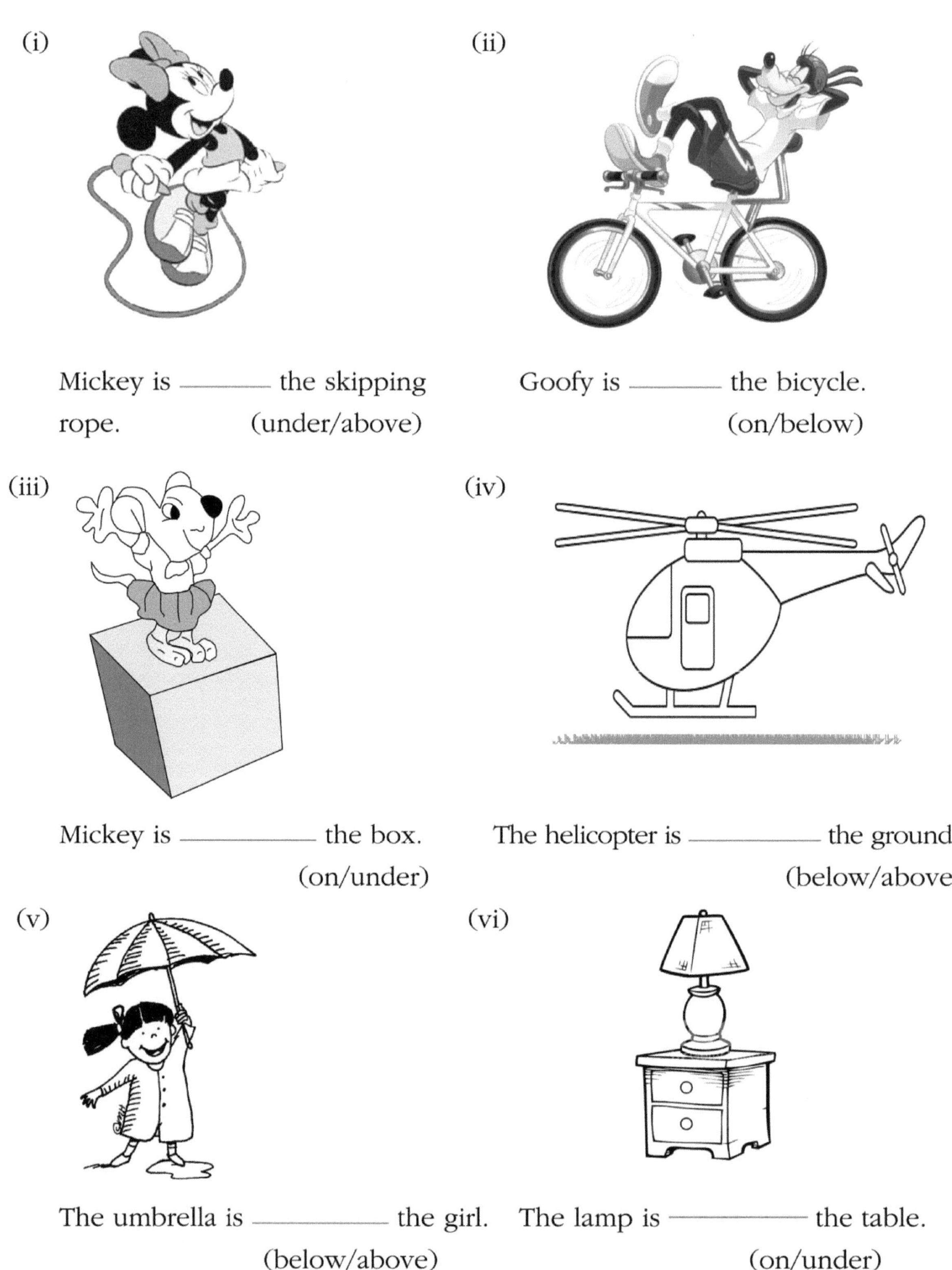

(i) Mickey is ______ the skipping rope. (under/above)

(ii) Goofy is ______ the bicycle. (on/below)

(iii) Mickey is ______ the box. (on/under)

(iv) The helicopter is ______ the ground. (below/above)

(v) The umbrella is ______ the girl. (below/above)

(vi) The lamp is ______ the table. (on/under)

8 Tick (✔) on ◯ (Circle) shapes and cross (✘) on ▭ (Rectangle) shapes.

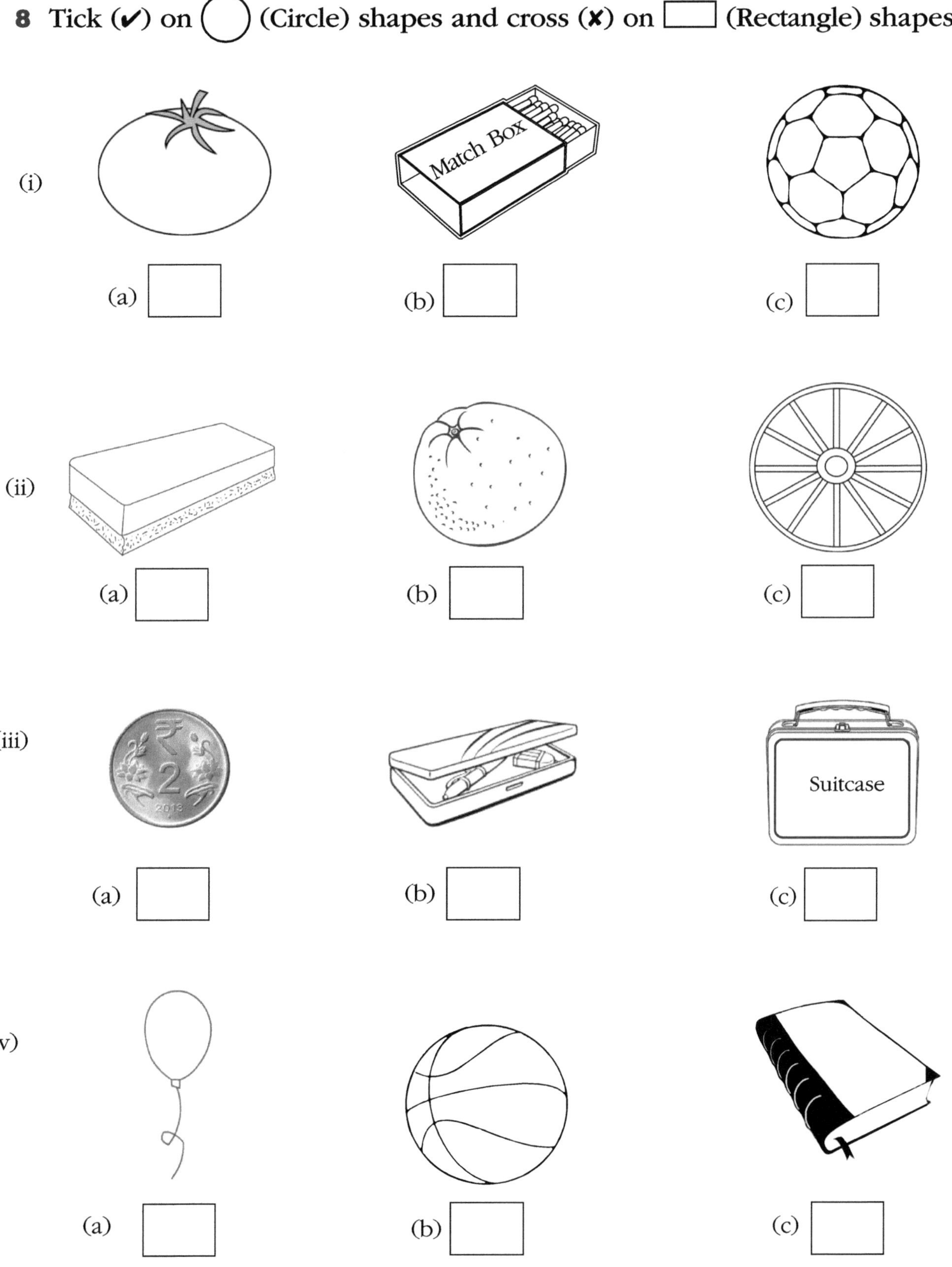

9 Given below are some figures numbered from (i) to (ix), colour these figures according to the instructions given below.

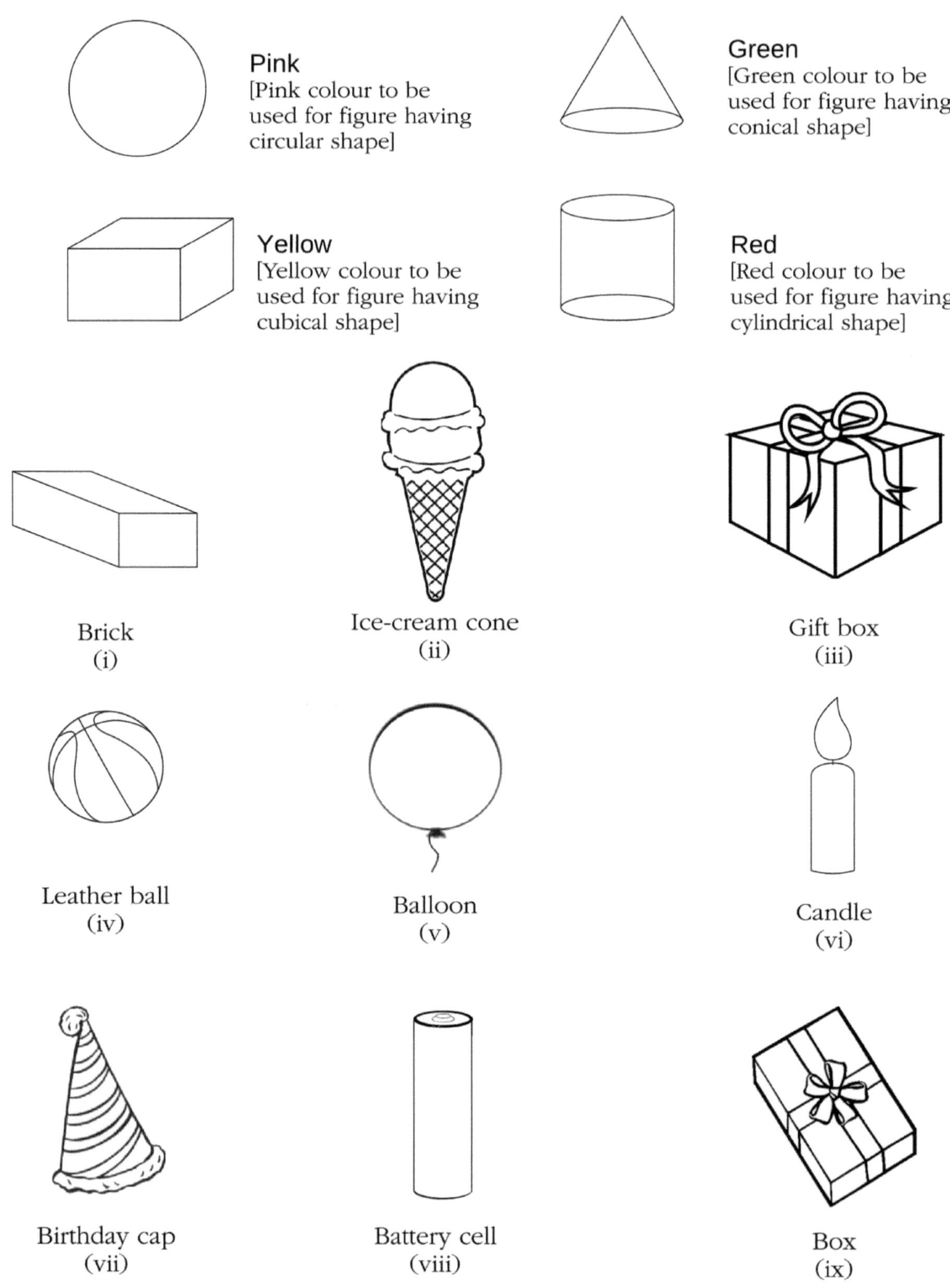

10 Match the shapes given in column I with similar shapes in column II.

Column I	Column II
(i)	(a) Match box
(ii)	(b)
(iii) Shoe box	(c) Chalk box
(iv)	(d)
(v)	(e)

11 (i) Tick (✓) the object which can slide.

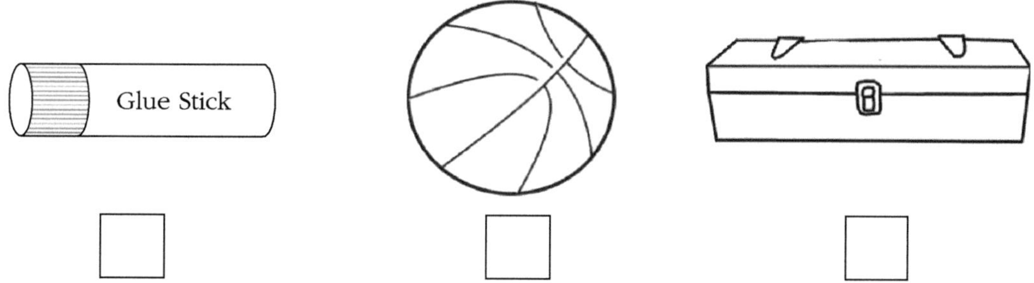

(ii) Tick (✔) the object which can roll.

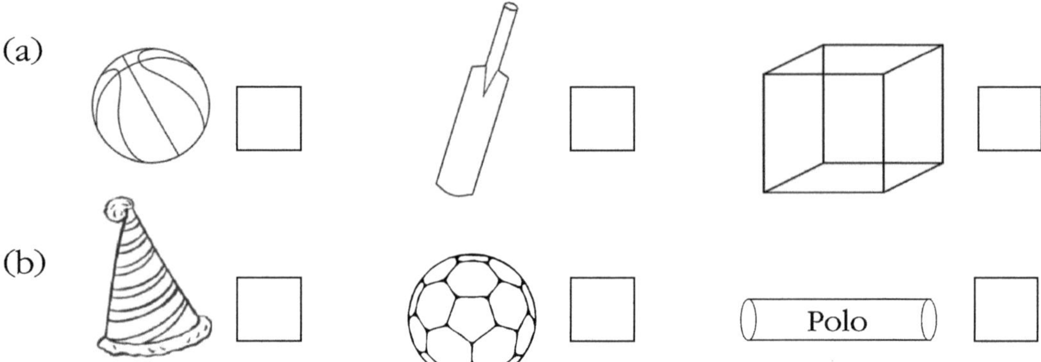

12 Colour the shapes of same size with same colour.

13 Match the similar shapes. One has been done for you.

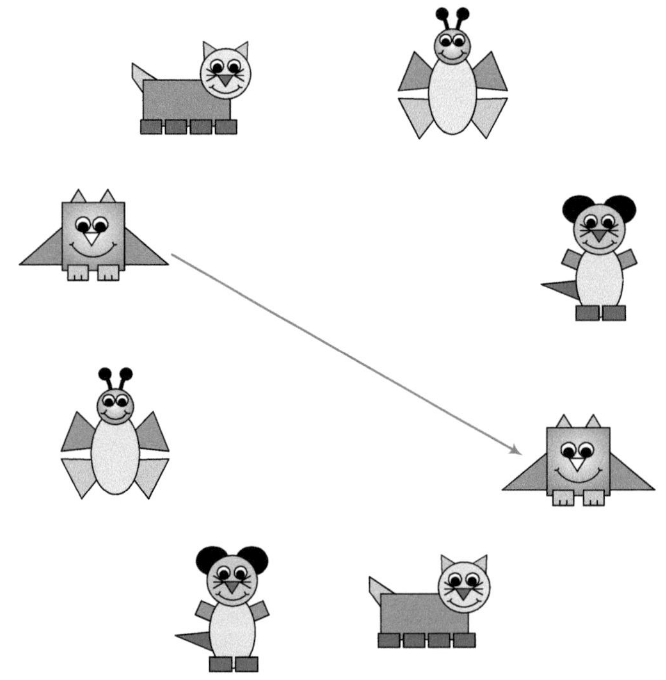

14 Colour the figures with the help of instructions given in each part.

(i) △ = Red, □ = Blue, ○ = Yellow, ▭ = Green

(ii) □ = Blue, △ = Green, ▭ = Red,

○ = Orange,

[Chapter 2]

Numbers from One to Nine

1 Draw the lines to show that each group has equal number of objects. One has been done for you.

(i)

(ii)

(iii)

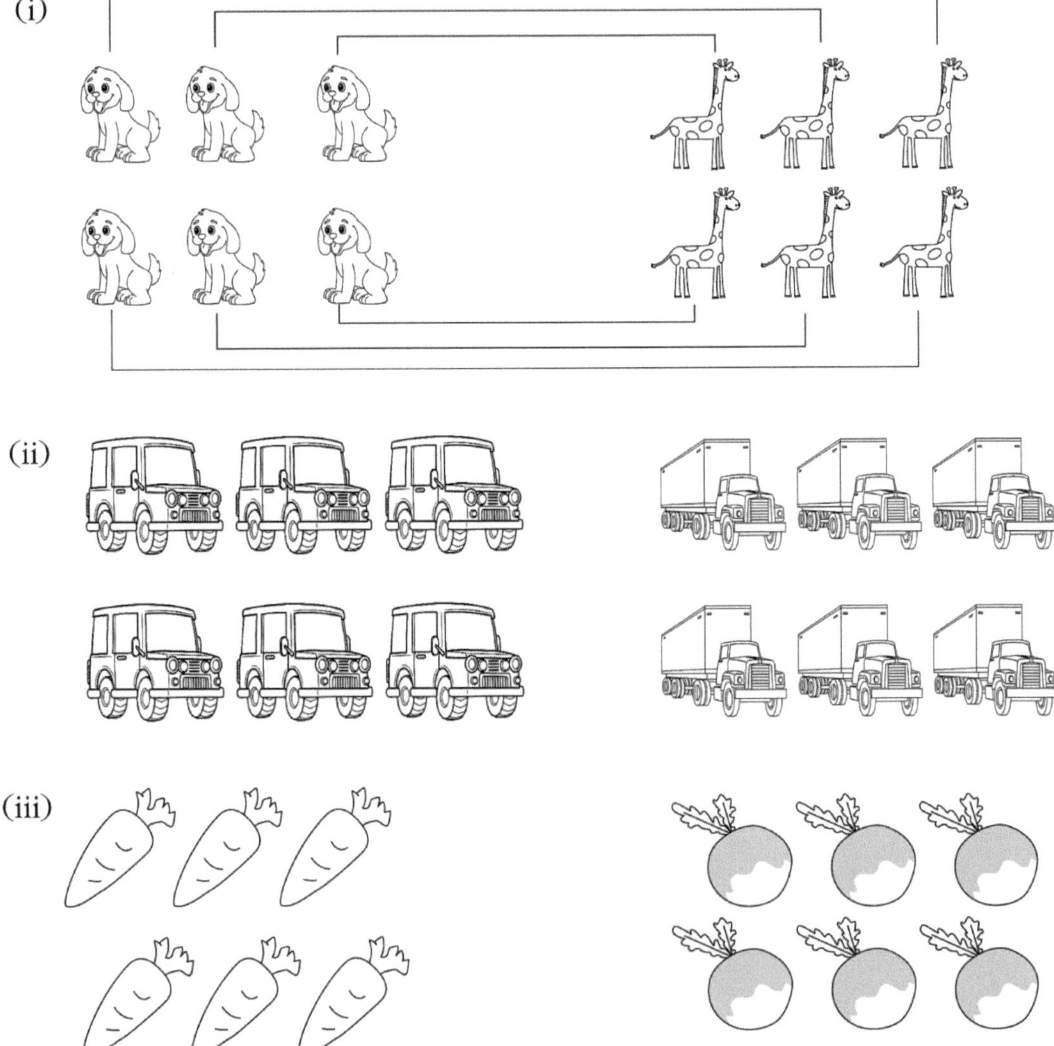

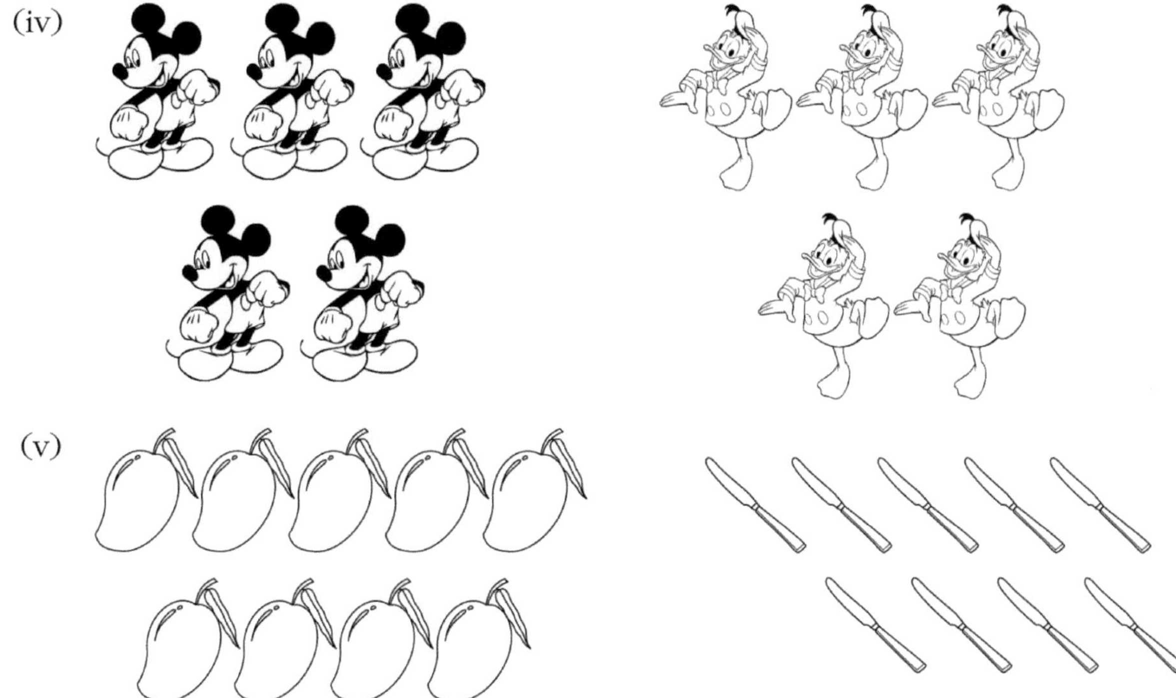

2 Count and write the number of birds alongwith the number name.

		Number	Name
(i)		= ________	________
(ii)		= ________	________
(iii)		= ________	________
(iv)		= ________	________
(v)		= ________	________
(vi)		= ________	________
(vii)		= ________	________
(viii)		= ________	________

3 Count the number of objects in each box and mark (✓) on the box having more objects and mark (✗) on the box having less objects.

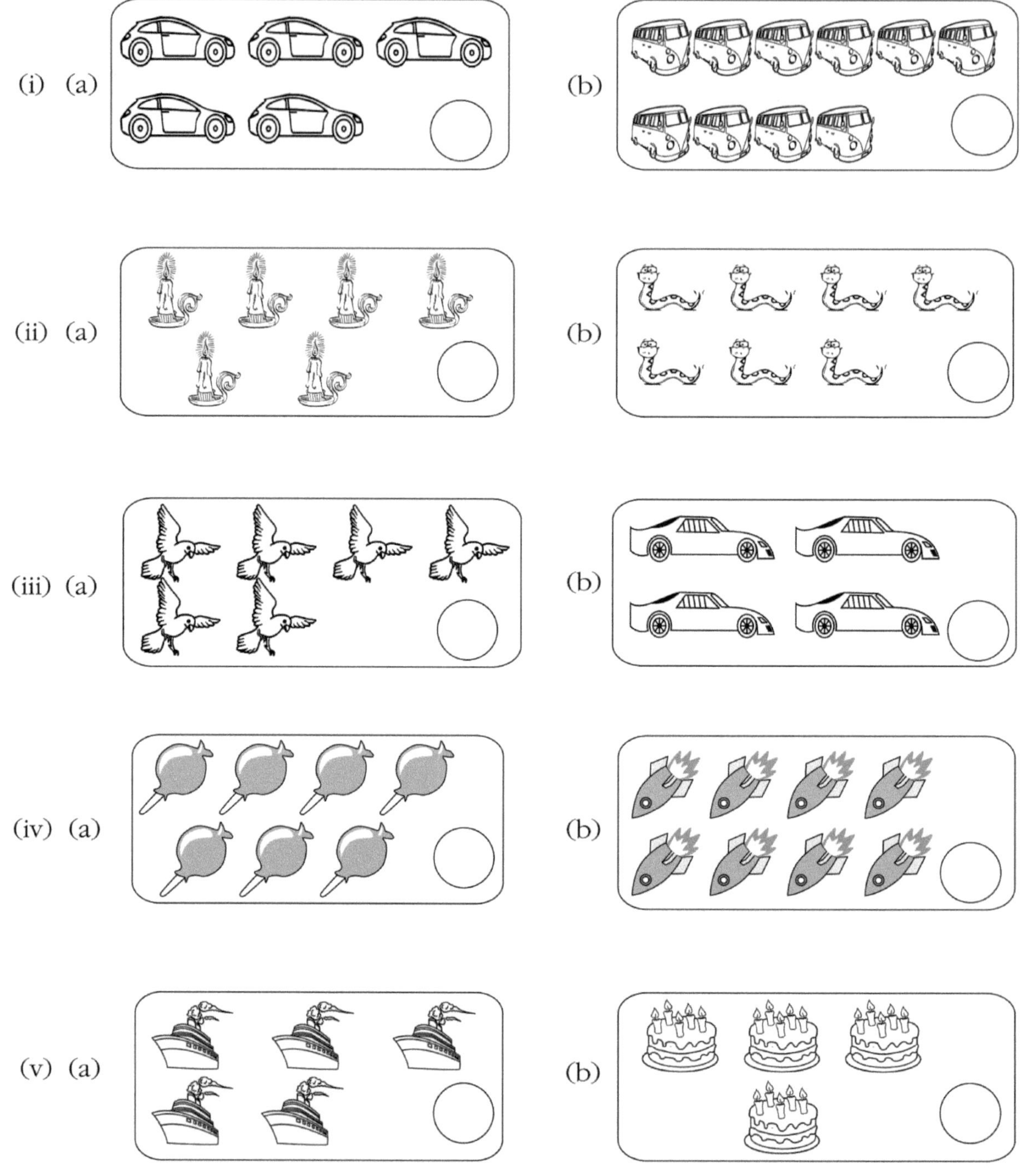

4 Count the number of circles given in column I and match them with the same number of objects given in column II.

Column I	Column II
(i) ○○○○○	(a) STOP STOP STOP 
(ii) ○○○○○○	(b) 
(iii) ○○○○	(c) 
(iv) ○○○○○○○	(d) 
(v) ○○○	(e) ☆☆☆☆☆ ☆☆ 

5 Join the dots in order to complete the figure and then colour it.

(i)

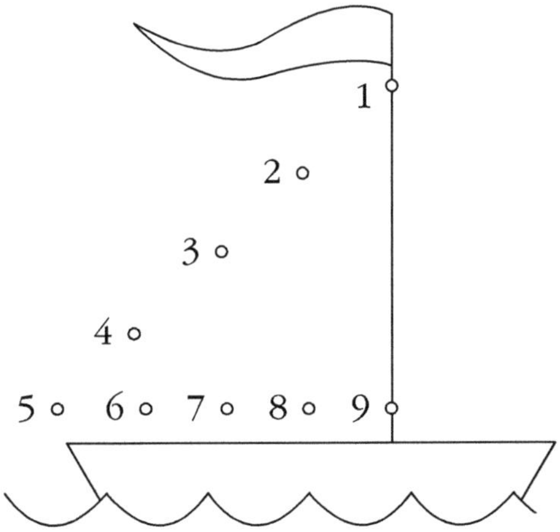

1
2 ∘
3 ∘
4 ∘
5 ∘ 6 ∘ 7 ∘ 8 ∘ 9

(ii)

•1
•2
•3
•4
5•
6•
7•
8•
9•

6 Count the number of objects given in column I and match them with the correct number given in column II.

	Column I		Column II
(i)		(a)	4
(ii)		(b)	6
(iii)	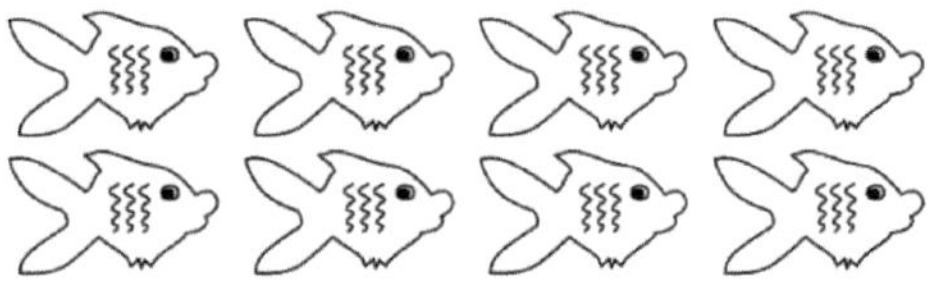	(c)	5
(iv)		(d)	7
(v)		(e)	9
(vi)		(f)	8
(vii)		(g)	3
(viii)	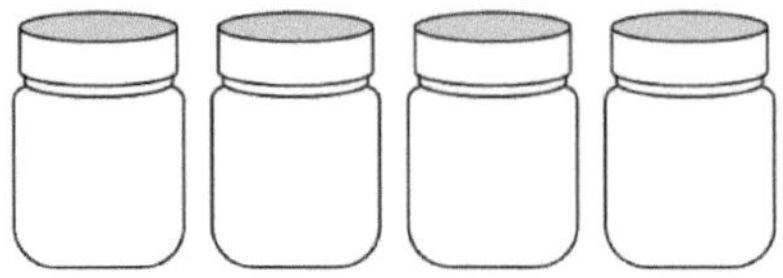	(h)	2

7 Make the group of objects according to the number given below each box. One has been done for you.

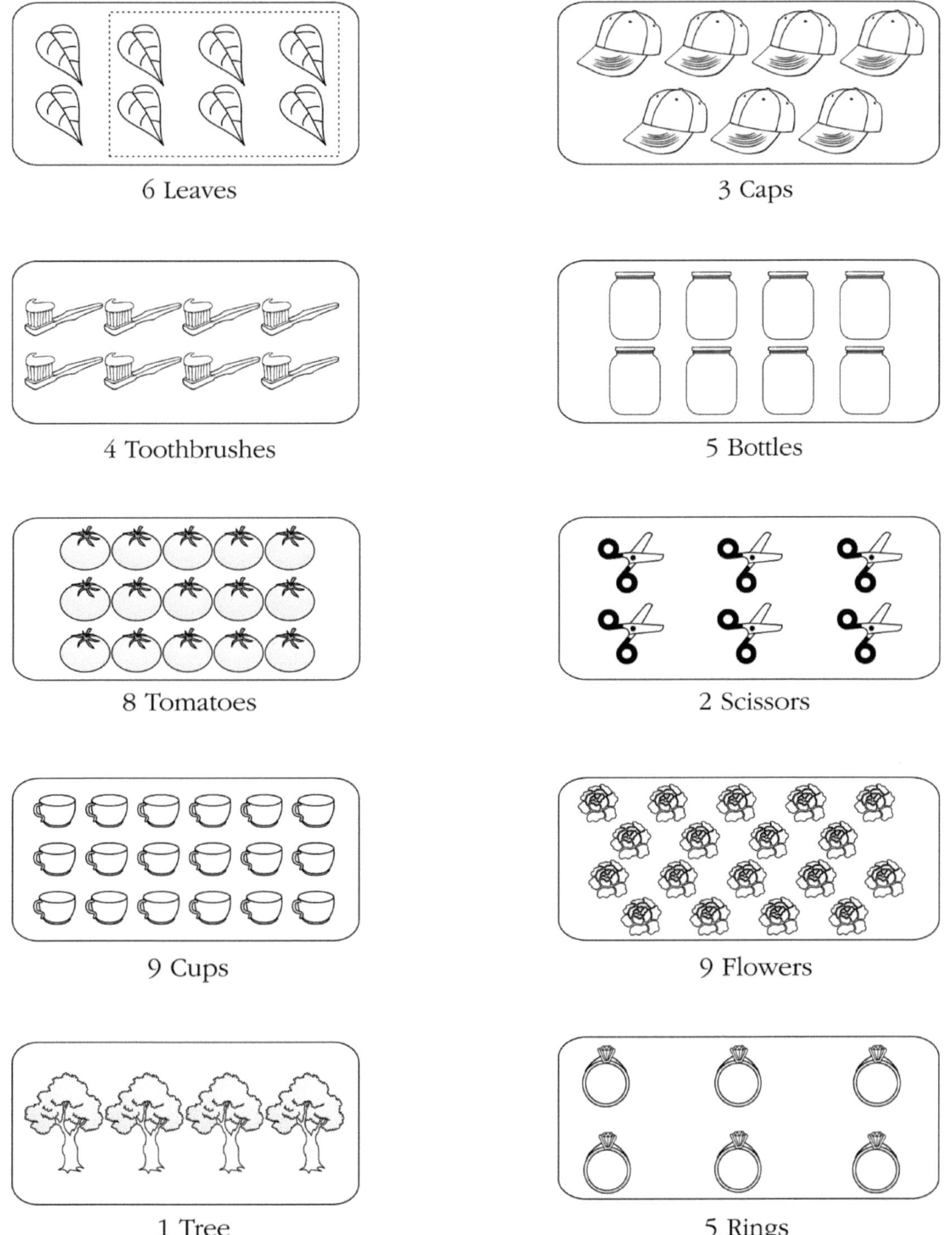

6 Leaves

3 Caps

4 Toothbrushes

5 Bottles

8 Tomatoes

2 Scissors

9 Cups

9 Flowers

1 Tree

5 Rings

8 Count and write the number of each animal.

(i) = ________ (ii) = ________

(iii) = ________ (iv) = ________

9 Write the missing number.

(i)

(ii)

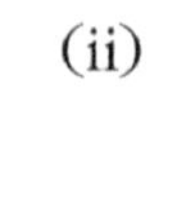

(iii)

(iv)

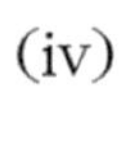

(v)

(vi)

10 Write the numbers before and after the given numbers.

Before				After
(i) ________	3	(ii)	8	________
(iii) ________	5	(iv)	2	________
(v) ________	8	(vi)	4	________
(vii) ________	9	(viii)	6	________
(ix) ________	7	(x)	1	________

11 Count and write the number of objects in each part.

(i)

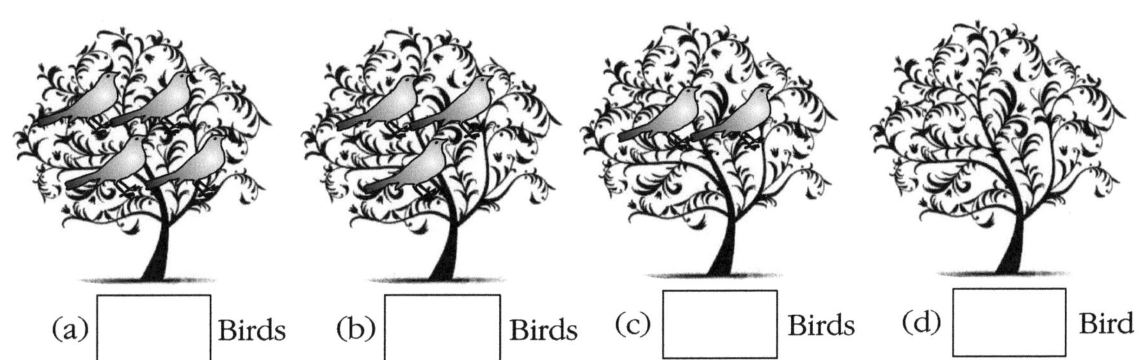

(a) ☐ Birds (b) ☐ Birds (c) ☐ Birds (d) ☐ Bird

(ii)

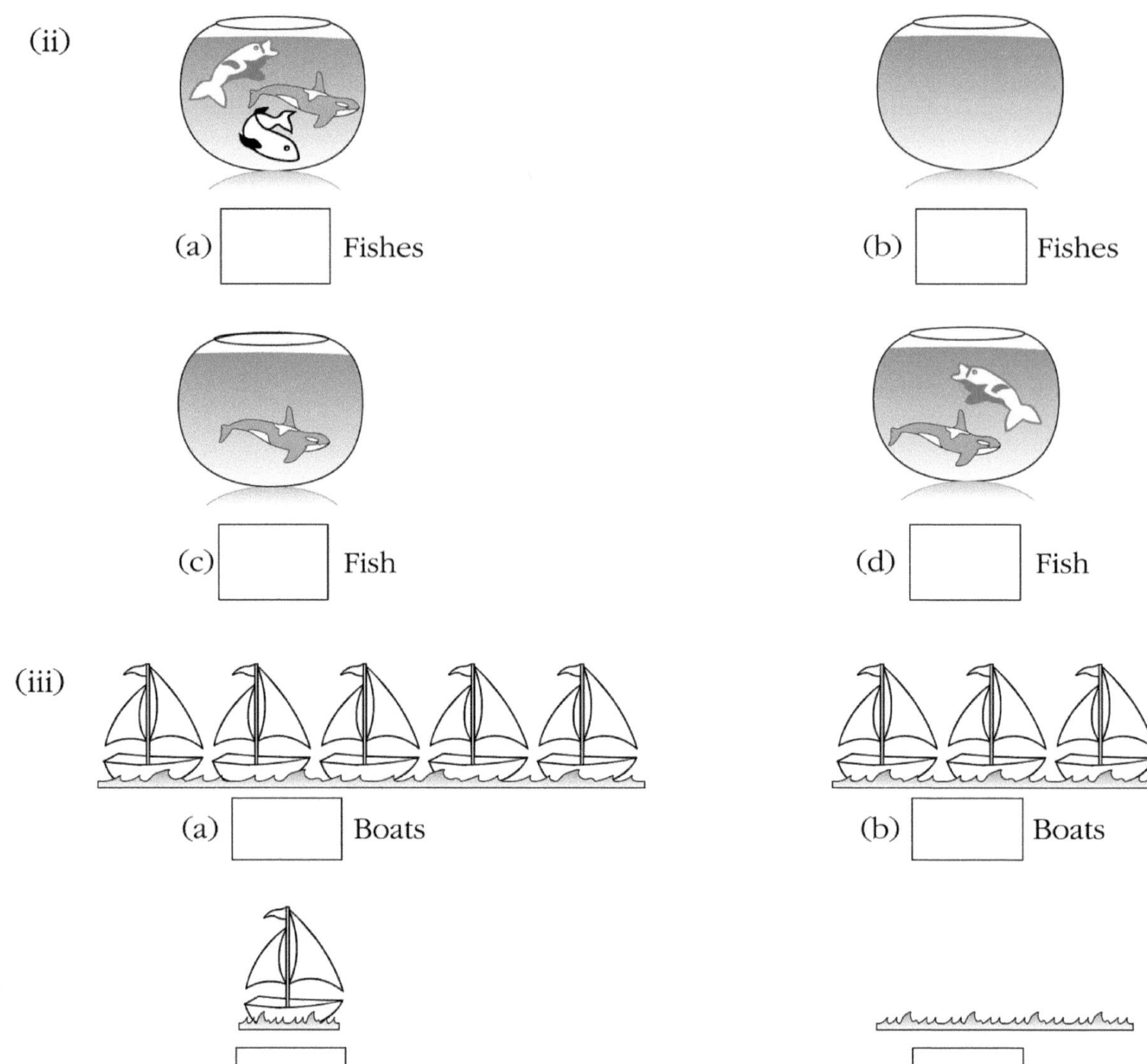

(a) ☐ Fishes

(b) ☐ Fishes

(c) ☐ Fish

(d) ☐ Fish

(iii)

(a) ☐ Boats

(b) ☐ Boats

(c) ☐ Boats

(d) ☐ Boats

Addition

1 Write the number which is one more than the number of objects given below. One has been done for you.

One more | Number

(i) + = 4

(ii) + = ______

(iii) + = ______

(iv) 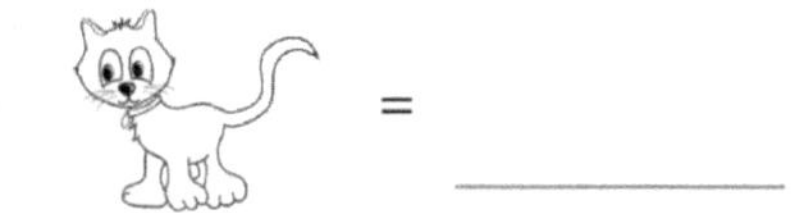

(v) 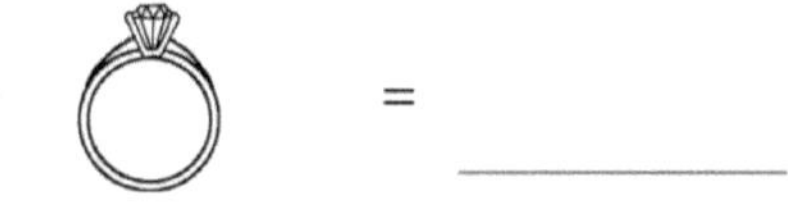

2 How many altogether? One has been done for you.

(i)  

[2] drinks and [1] drink = [3] drinks.

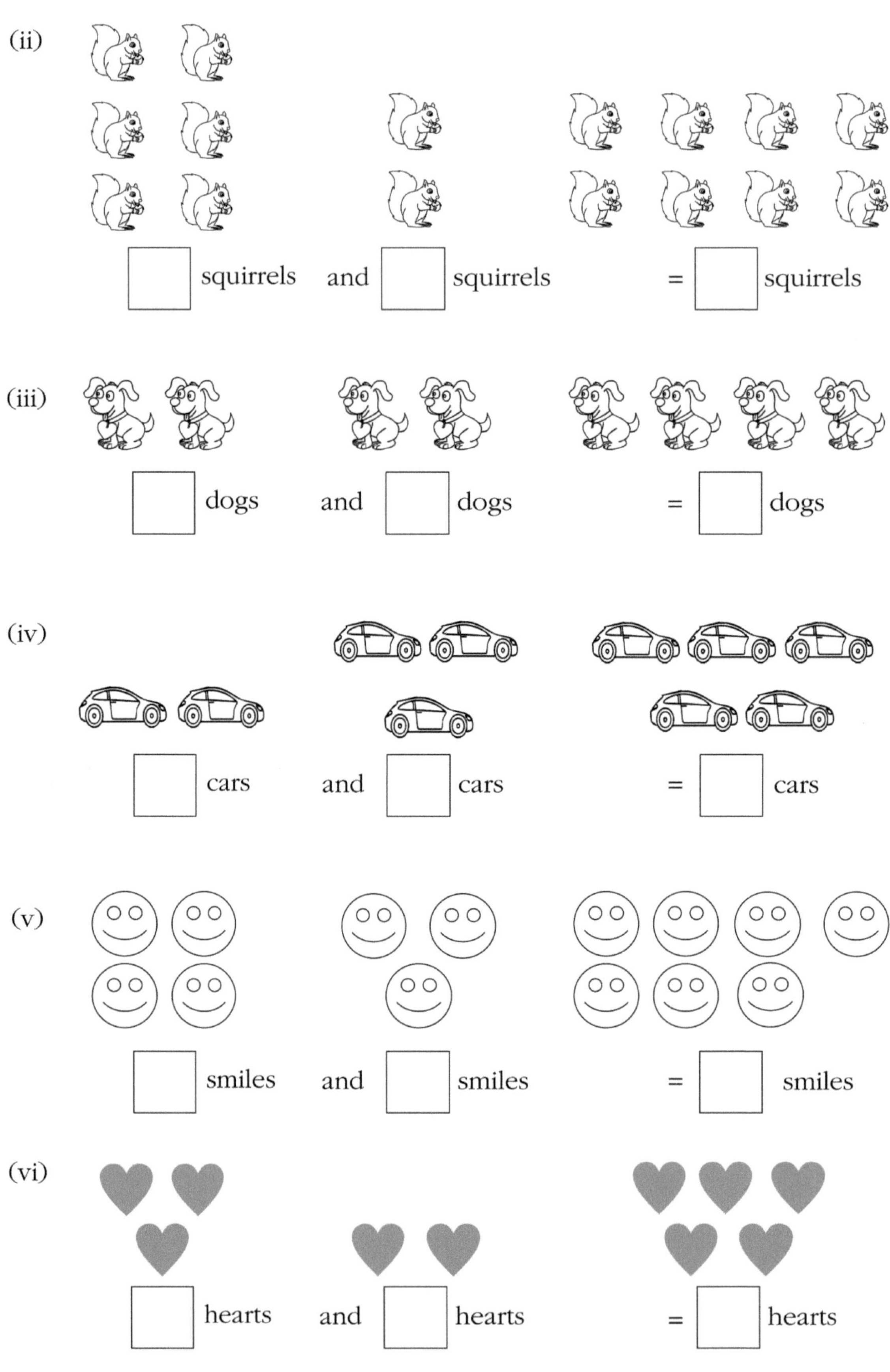
(ii)
squirrels and squirrels = squirrels
(iii)
dogs and dogs = dogs
(iv)
cars and cars = cars
(v)
smiles and smiles = smiles
(vi)
hearts and hearts = hearts

3 Count the objects and write their number in the boxes given below. Also, add them and write the result in the last box.

(i) ☐ + ☐ = ☐

(ii) ☐ + ☐ = ☐

(iii) ☐ + ☐ = ☐

(iv) ☐ + ☐ = ☐

(v) ☐ + ☐ = ☐

(vi)

☐ + ☐ = ☐

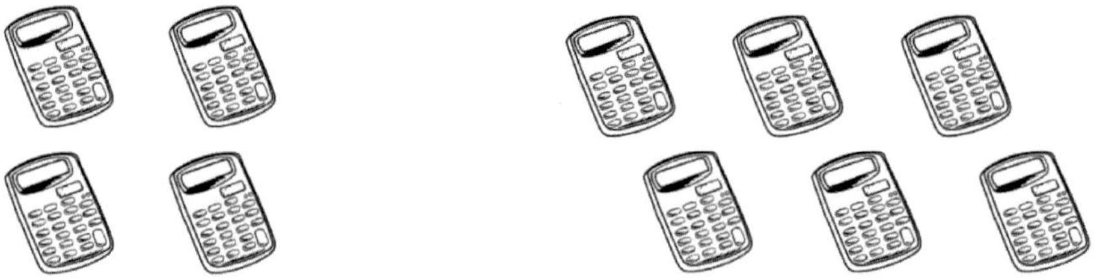

(vii)

☐ + ☐ = ☐

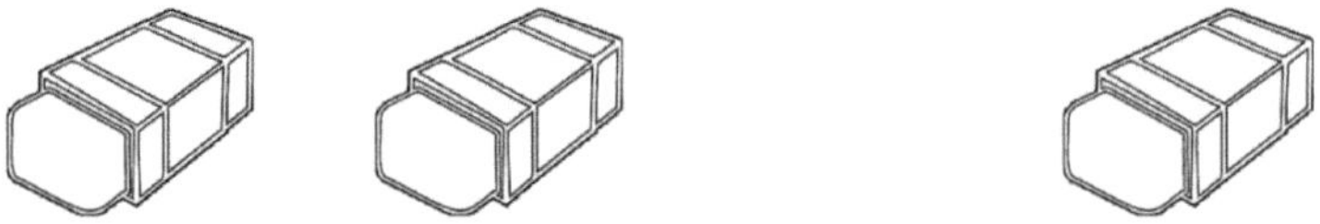

(viii)

☐ + ☐ = ☐

4 Match the following. One has been done for you.

(i) (a) 4 + 3

(ii) (b) 1 + 5

(iii) (c) 2 + 3

(iv) (d) 7 + 1

(v) (e) 3 + 6

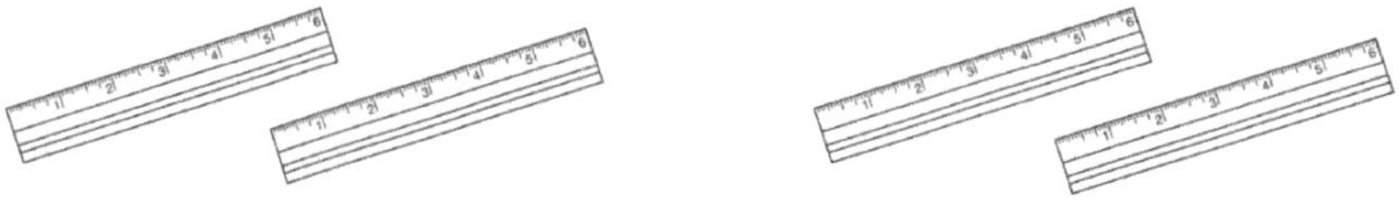

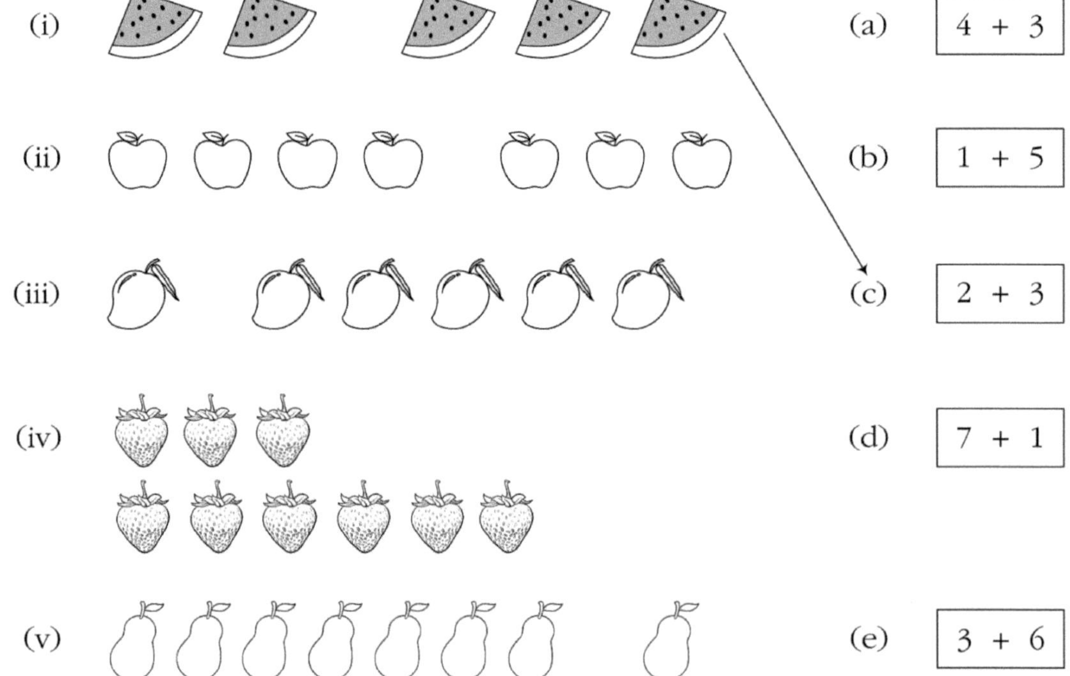

5 Add the given objects and circle the correct answer in the box. One has been done for you.

(i)  +  = 2, 3, (4)

(ii)  +  = 2, 3, 4

(iii)  +  = 4, 5, 6

(iv)  +  = 7, 8, 9

(v)  +  = 7, 8, 9

(vi)  +  = 4, 5, 6

6 Add and match. One has been done for you.

(i) 3 + 1	I. ★★★ ★★★ ★	(a) 3 + 5
(ii) 6 + 2	II. ★★★ ★★	(b) 4 + 1
(iii) 3 + 4	III. ★★★	(c) 2 + 2
(iv) 3 + 6	IV. ★★★ ★	(d) 1 + 8
(v) 5 + 0	V. ★★★ ★★★ ★★	(e) 2 + 5
(vi) 1 + 2	VI. ★★★ ★★★ ★★★	(f) 2 + 1

7 Add the numbers and fill the boxes.

(i) $4 + 3 = \square$

(ii) $7 + 1 = \square$

(iii) $2 + 4 = \square$

(iv) $3 + 5 = \square$

(v) $4 + 0 = \square$

(vi) $3 + 6 = \square$

(vii) $7 + 2 = \square$

(viii) $1 + 8 = \square$

(ix) $0 + 8 = \square$

(x) $3 + 2 = \square$

(xi) $5 + 4 = \square$

(xii) $2 + 5 = \square$

8 Write the missing numerals.

(i) $\square + \square = 7$

(ii) $\square + \square = 6$

(iii) $\square + \square = 3$

(iv) $\square + \square = 9$

(v) $\square + \square = 5$

(vi) $\square + \square = 4$

(vii) $\square + \square = 1$

(viii) $\square + \square = 8$

9 In each tree, circle any two leaves that have a sum shown on its stem. One has been done for you.

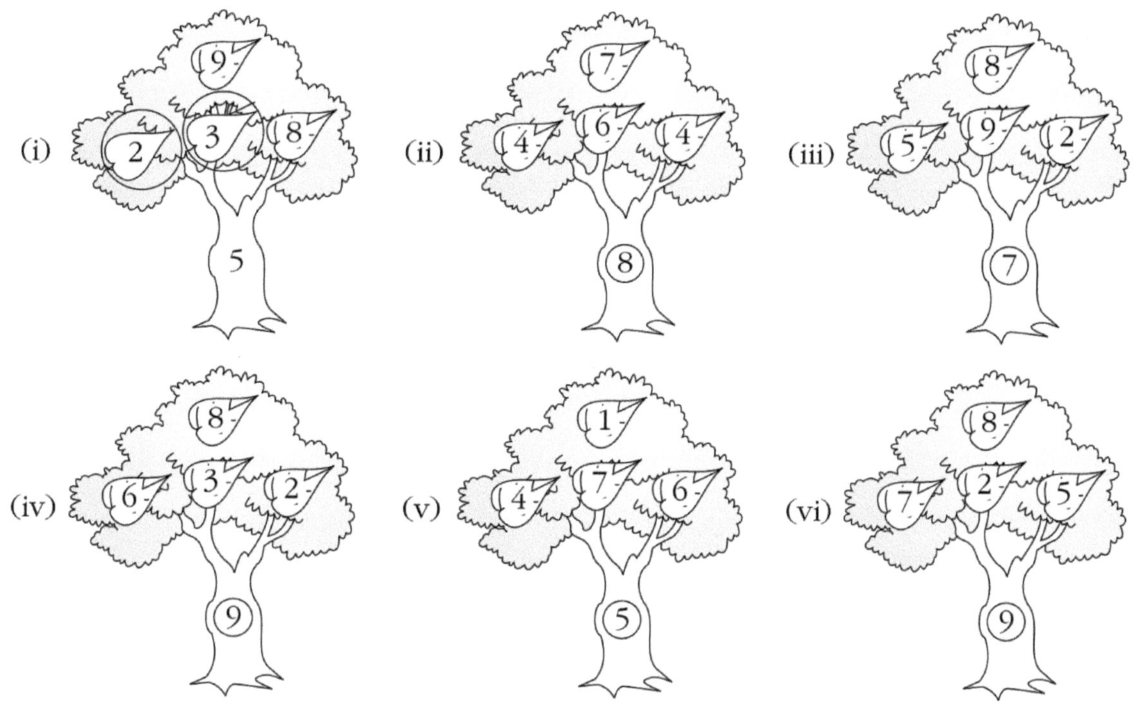

10 Problems based on addition.

(i) There are 5 frogs. 3 more frogs came. How many altogether?

(ii) Jack has 4 flowers. His friend gave him 3 more. How many flowers does he have now?

(iii) Tom had 7 pens. John had 1 pen. How many pens they both had?

Chapter 4

Subtraction

1 Fill the boxes. One has been done for you.

(i)

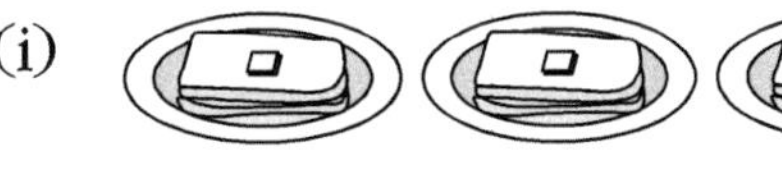

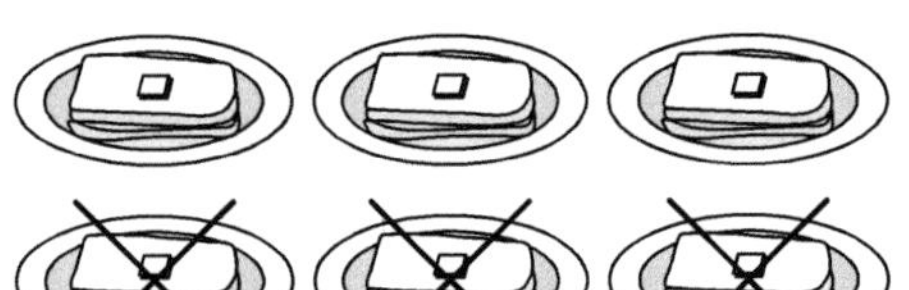

From [9] Take away [3] Left [6]

[9] – [3] = [6]

(ii)

From [ ] Take away [ ] Left [ ]

[ ] – [ ] = [ ]

(iii)

From [ ] Take away [ ] Left [ ]

[ ] – [ ] = [ ]

(iv)

From [ ] Take away [ ] Left [ ]

[ ] – [ ] = [ ]

(v)

From ☐ Take away ☐ Left ☐

☐ – ☐ = ☐

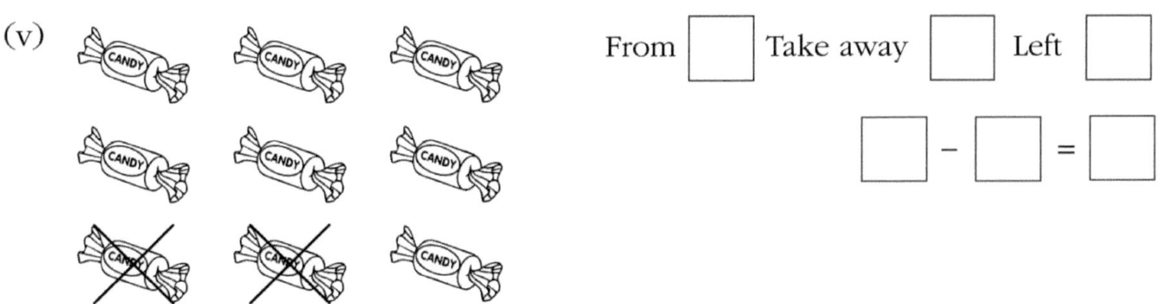

2 **Count and subtract. One has been done for you.**

(i)

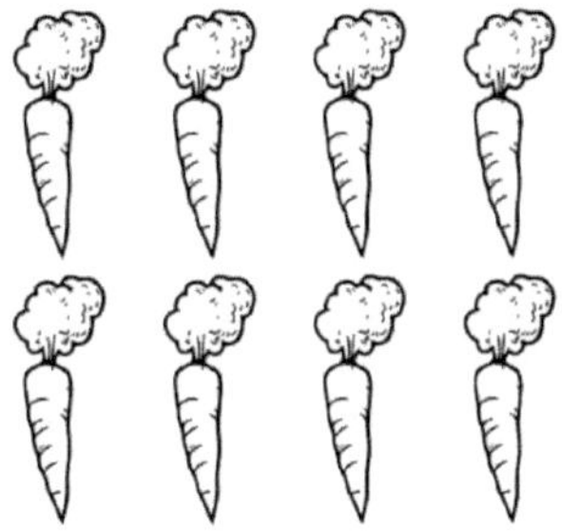

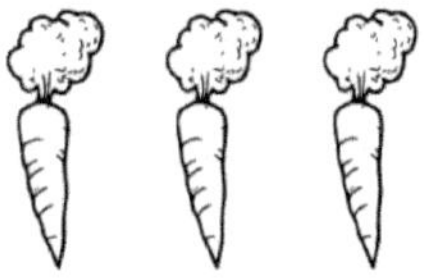

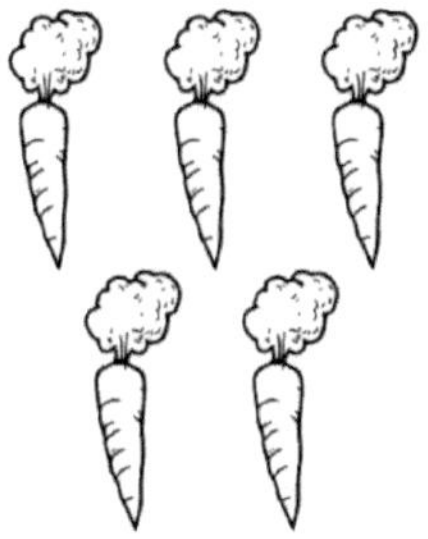

8 – 3 = 5

(ii)

☐ – ☐ = ☐

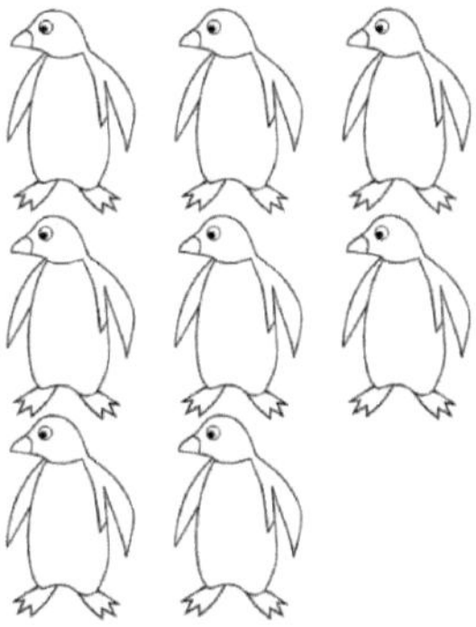

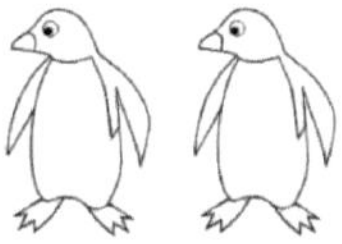

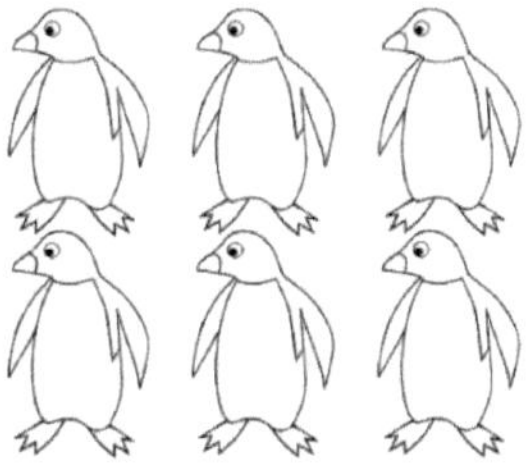

(iii)

☐ – ☐ = ☐

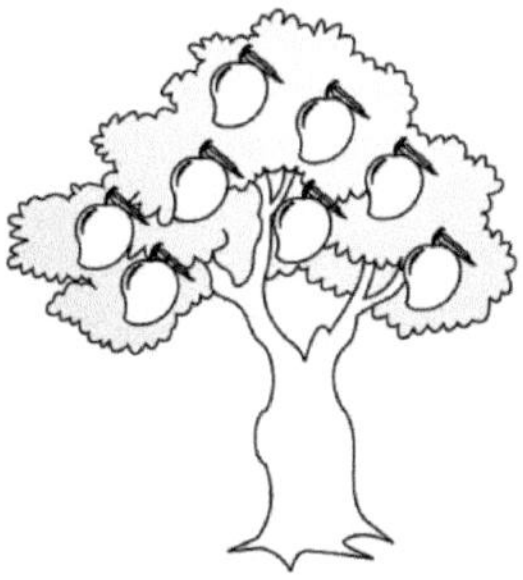

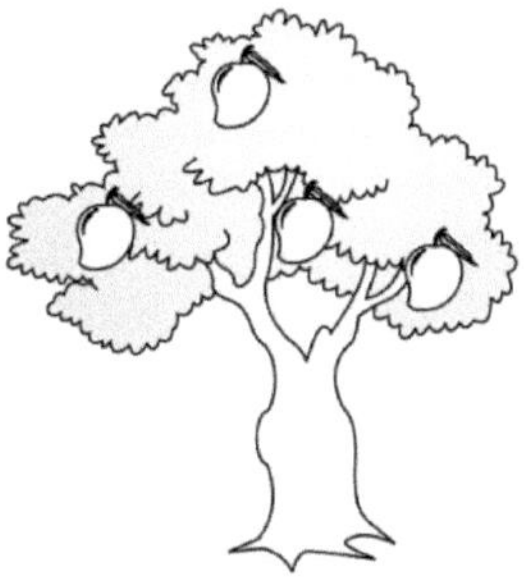

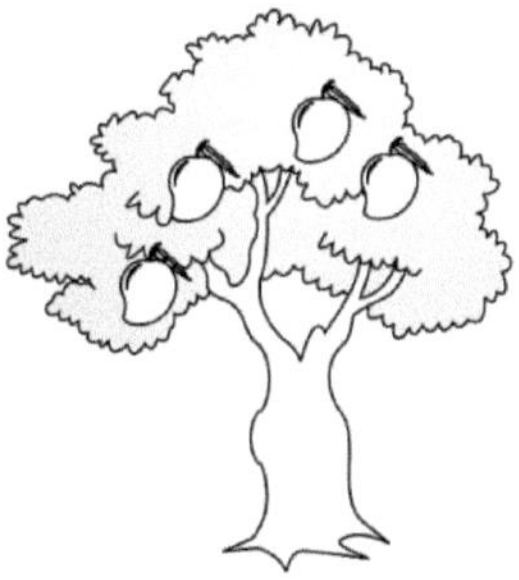

(iv)  − 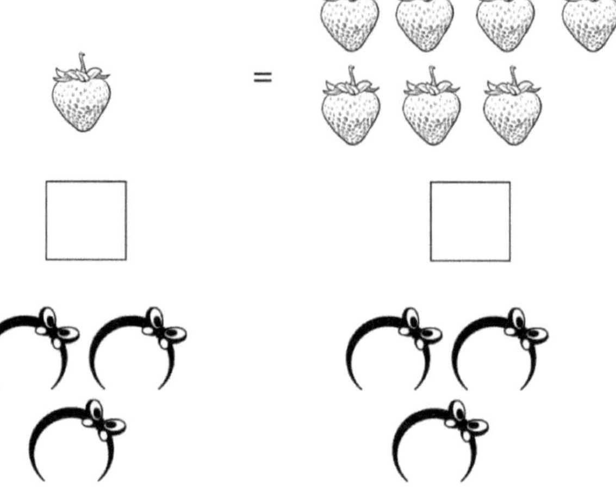 =

☐ ☐ ☐

(v) 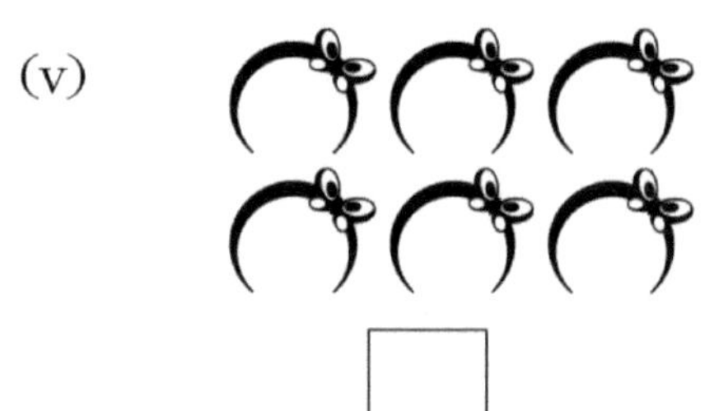 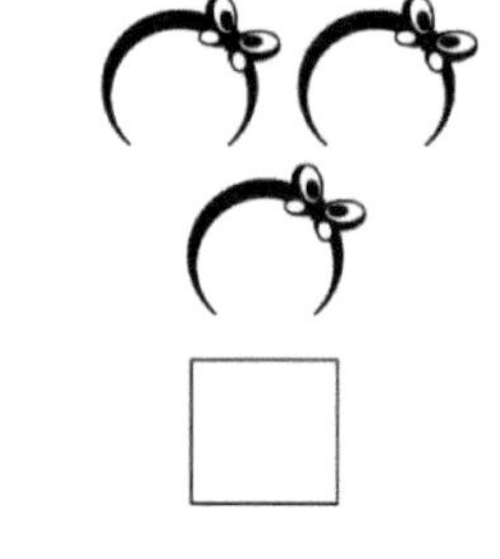 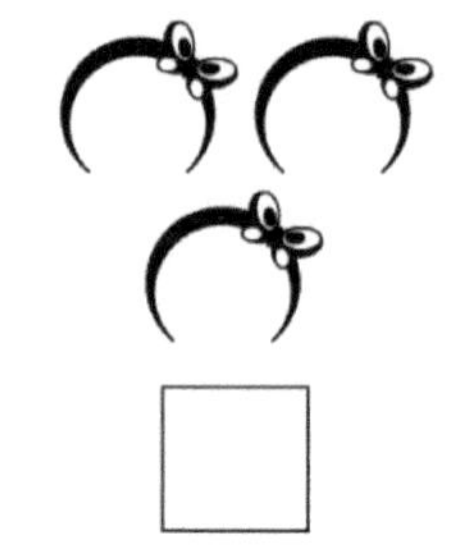

☐ − ☐ = ☐

3 Subtract and match. One has been done for you.

(i)	8 − 2 =	0	(vi)	9 − 2 =
		1		
(ii)	9 − 9 =	2	(vii)	9 − 0 =
		3		
(iii)	6 − 5 =	4	(viii)	9 − 5 =
		5		
(iv)	6 − 4 =	6	(ix)	8 − 0 =
		7		
(v)	5 − 2 =	8	(x)	6 − 1 =
		9		

4 Solve the following.

(i) $\begin{array}{r} 9 \\ -4 \\ \hline \\ \hline \end{array}$ (ii) $\begin{array}{r} 7 \\ -3 \\ \hline \\ \hline \end{array}$ (iii) $\begin{array}{r} 9 \\ -7 \\ \hline \\ \hline \end{array}$ (iv) $\begin{array}{r} 6 \\ -3 \\ \hline \\ \hline \end{array}$

5 Write the missing numbers.

(i) 7 – 3 = ___ (ii) ___ – 6 = 3

(iii) 5 – ___ = 1 (iv) ___ – 3 = 5

(v) 9 – ___ = 9 (vi) 3 – 0 = ___

(vii) 7 – ___ = 5 (viii) 5 – ___ = 0

(ix) ___ – 0 = 8

6 Subtract and fill in the domino. One has been done for you.

(i) 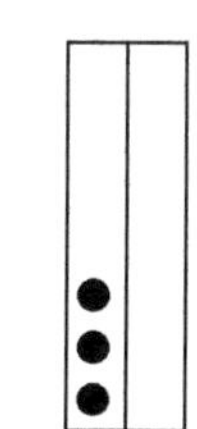 – =

(ii) – =

(iii) 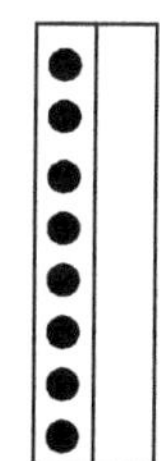 – =

(iv) 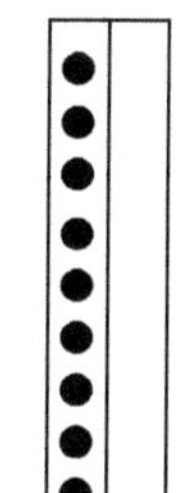 – =

(v) 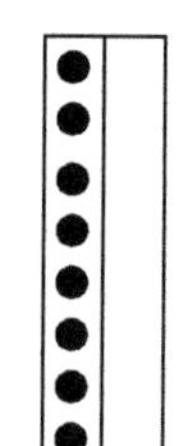 – 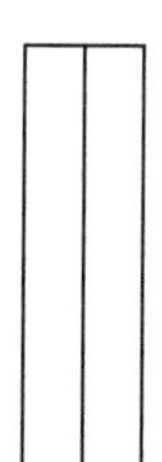 =

7 Problems based on subtraction.

(i) Julie has 9 dolls. She gave 4 dolls to Anna. How many dolls does Julie have now?

____

____

(ii) James has 7 toy cars. 3 toy cars broke. How many toy cars are left with him?

____

____

(iii) John's mom buys 8 apples. John eats some of them. There are 3 left. How many apples did John eat?

____

____

(iv) Marry has 9 marbles. She lost 6 of them. How many marbles does she have now?

____

____

(v) Rohan bought 8 bats. Some of them broke. 5 bats are left now. How many bats broke?

____

____

[Chapter 5]

Numbers from Ten to Twenty

1 Make a group of objects as indicated in each part. One has been done for you.

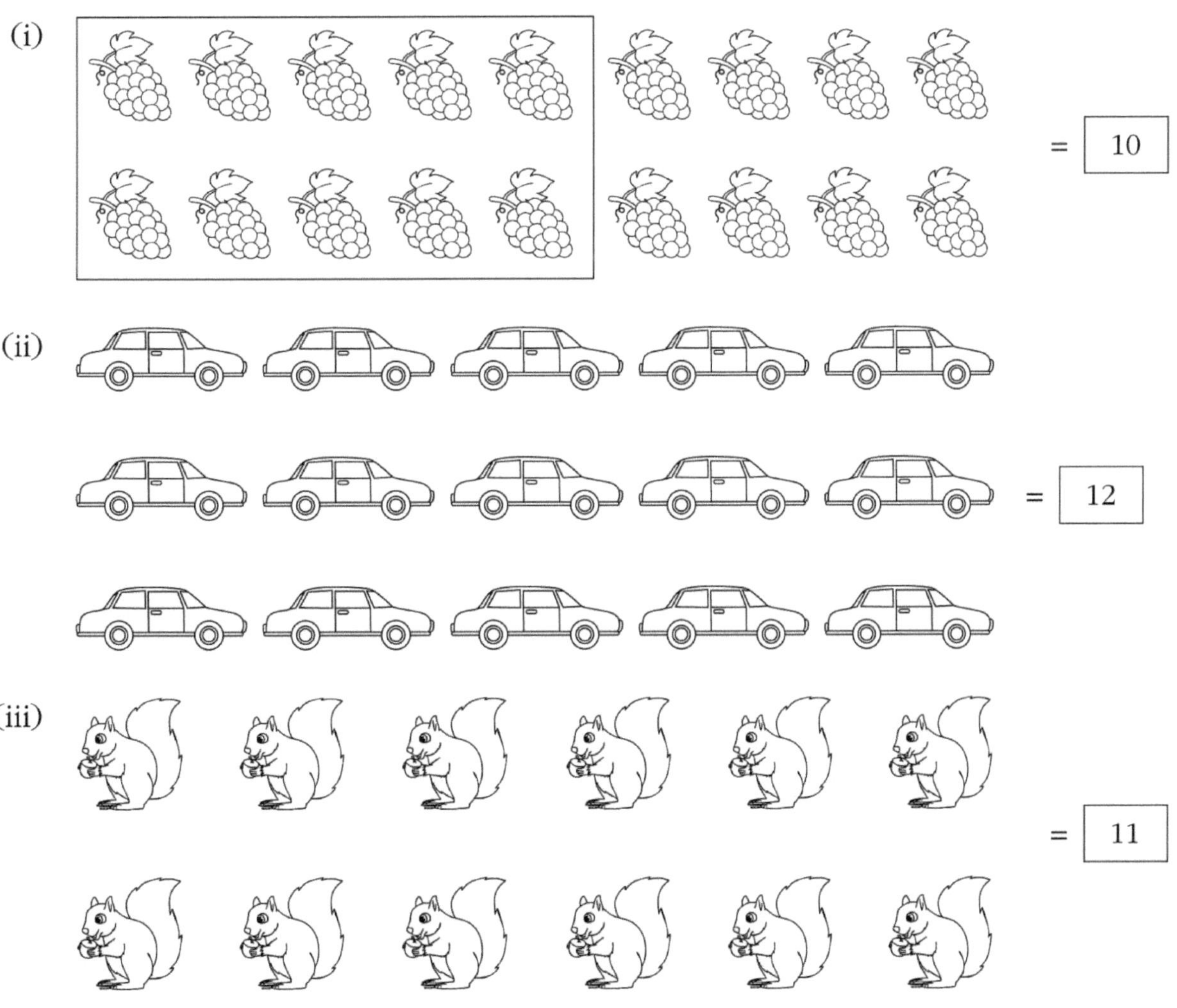

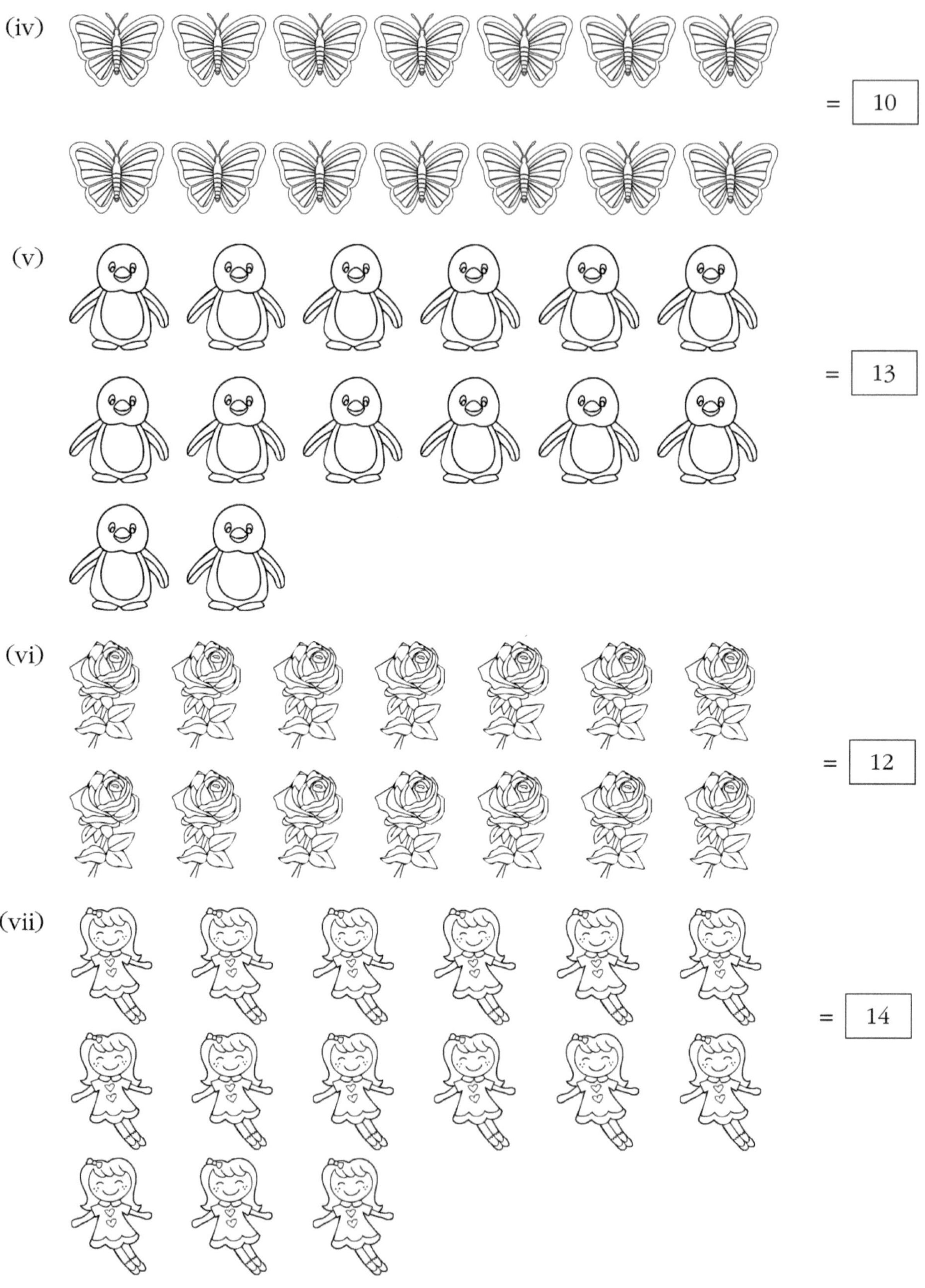
(iv)
= 10
(v)
= 13
(vi)
= 12
(vii)
= 14

2 Make a group of 10 and write the numbers. One has been done for you.

(i)

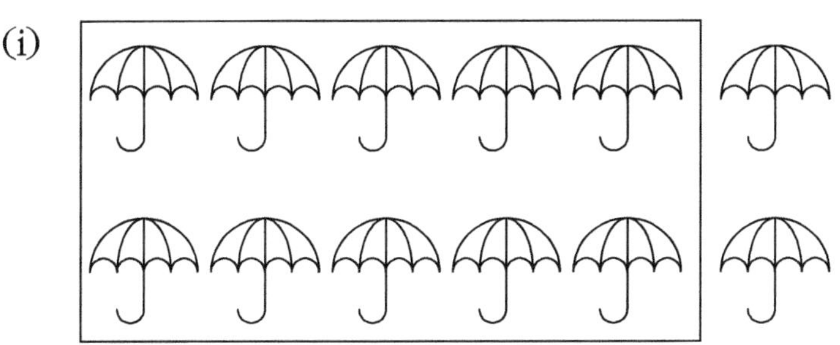

Tens	Ones
1	2

10 + 2 = 12

(ii)

Tens	Ones

☐ + ☐ = ☐

(iii)

Tens	Ones

☐ + ☐ = ☐

(iv)

Tens	Ones

☐ + ☐ = ☐

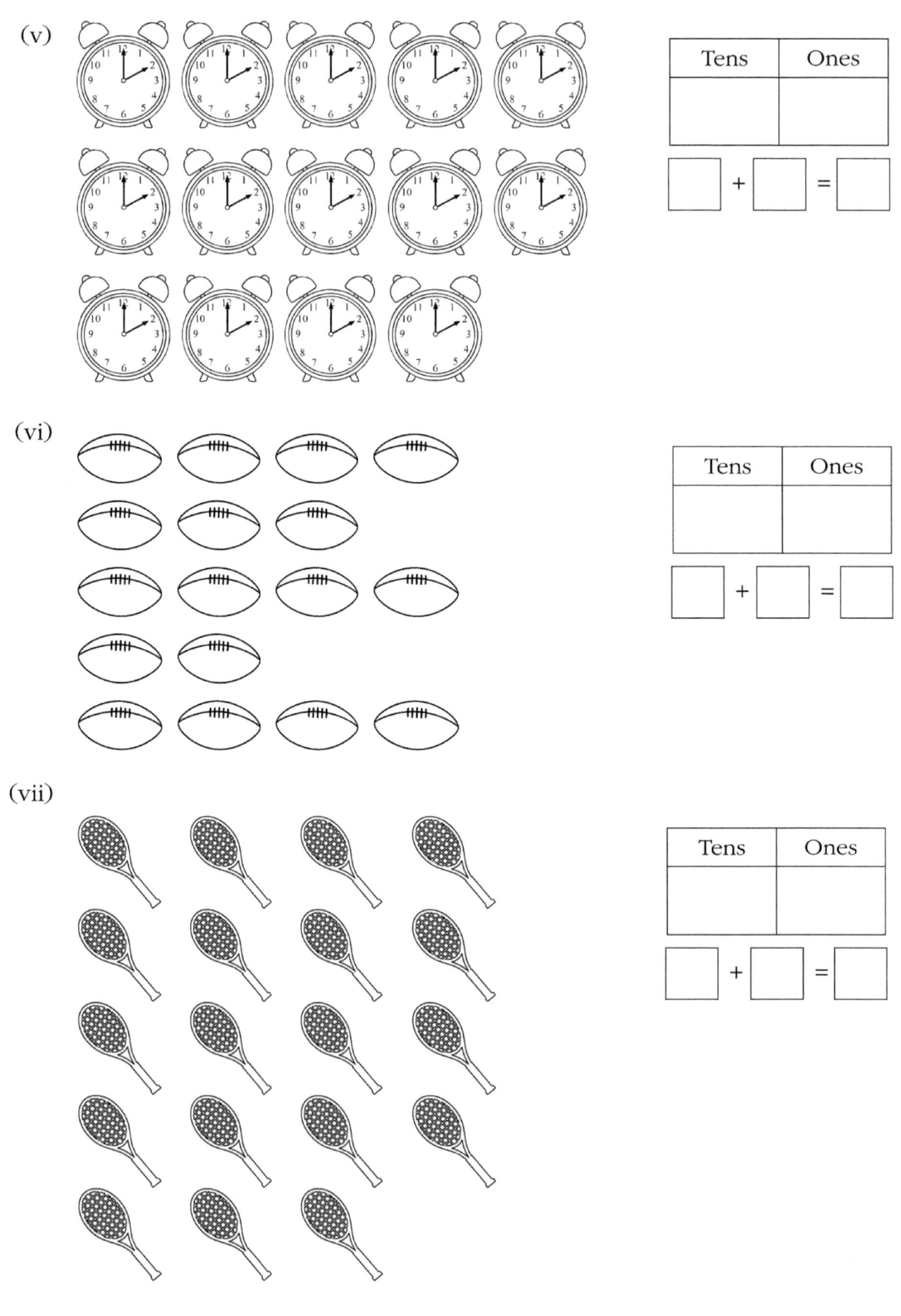
(v)
Tens
Ones
+
=
(vi)
Tens
Ones
+
=
(vii)
Tens
Ones
+
=

3 Fill in the blanks. One has been done for you.

(i) 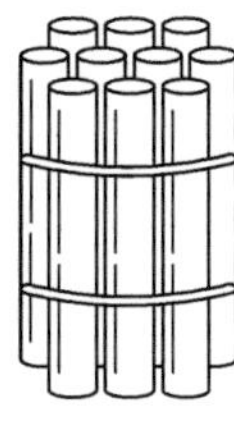 + 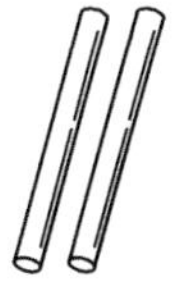 = 12

10 2

(ii) 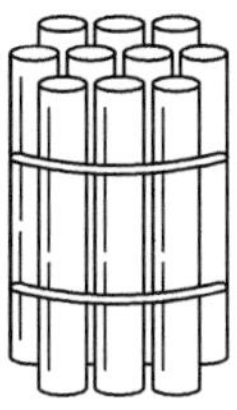 + 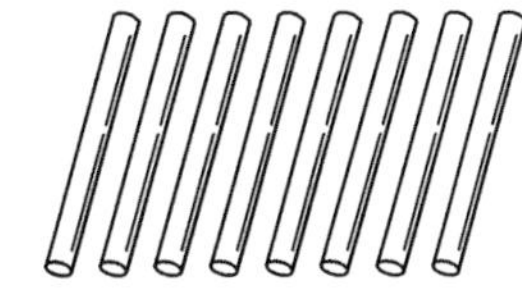 = ☐

10 8

(iii) 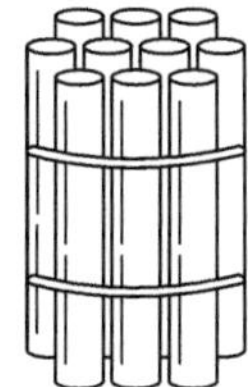 +  = ☐

10 4

(iv) 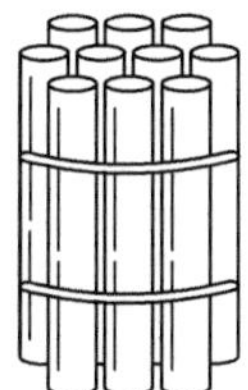 + 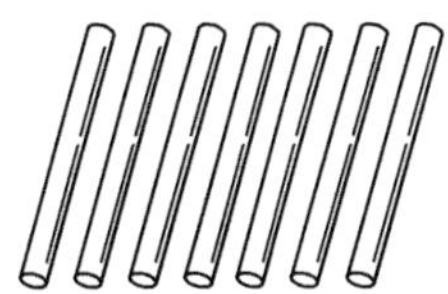 = ☐

10 7

(v) 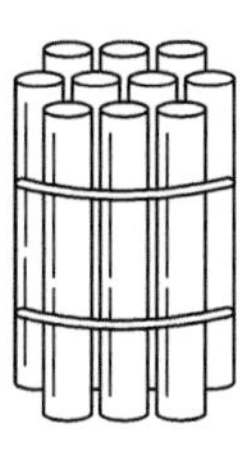 + 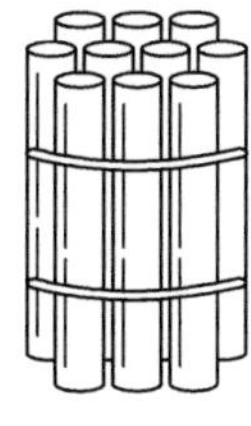 = ☐

10 10

4 **Write the next three numbers and their names.**

10 ______ ______ ______ Ten ______ ______ ______

11 ______ ______ ______ Eleven ______ ______ ______

12 ______ ______ ______ Twelve ______ ______ ______

13 ______ ______ ______ Thirteen ______ ______ ______

14 ______ ______ ______ Fourteen ______ ______ ______

15 ______ ______ ______ Fifteen ______ ______ ______

16 ______ ______ ______ Sixteen ______ ______ ______

17 ______ ______ ______ Seventeen ______ ______ ______

5 **Write the numbers before/after the given numbers.**

(i)

(ii)

(iii)

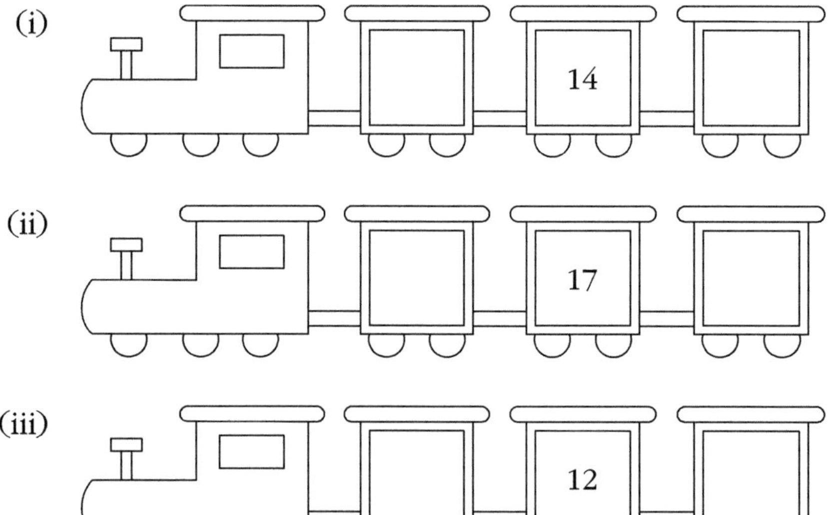

(iv)

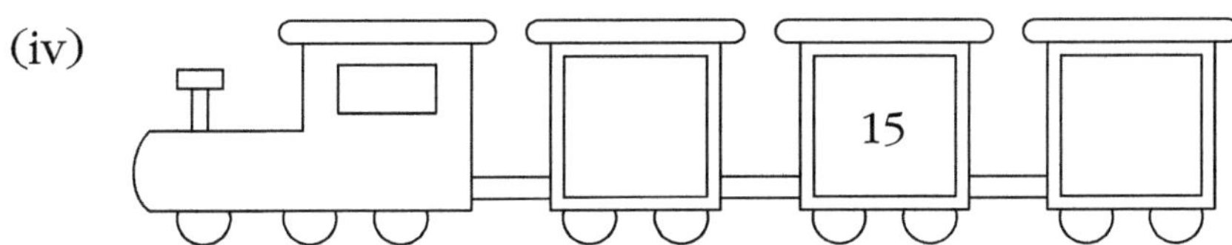

(v)

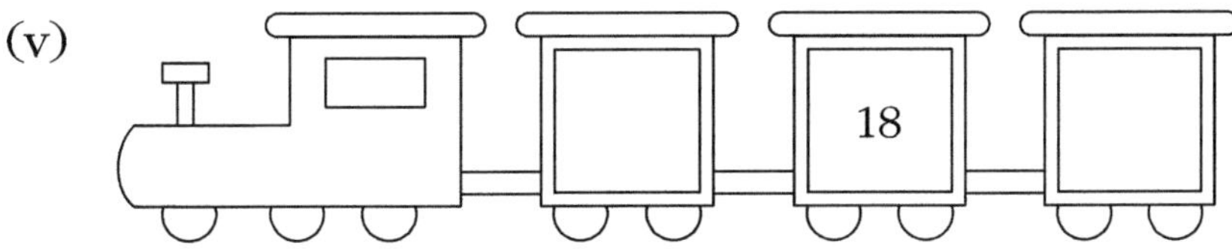

(vi)

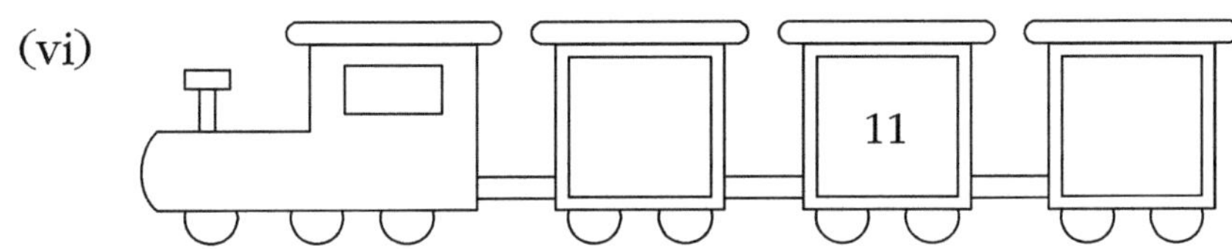

6 Write the numbers between the given two numbers.

(i)

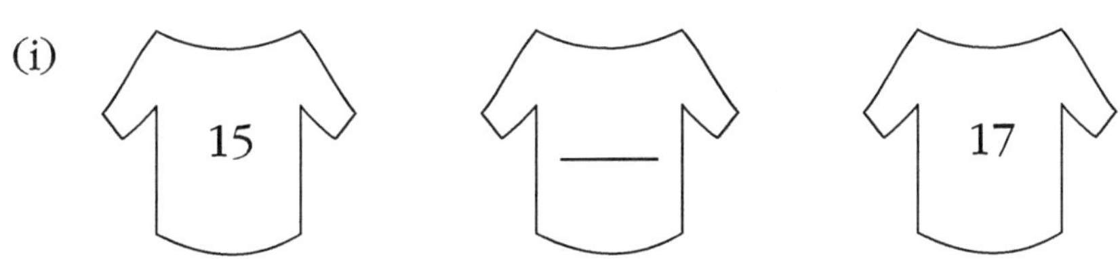

(ii)

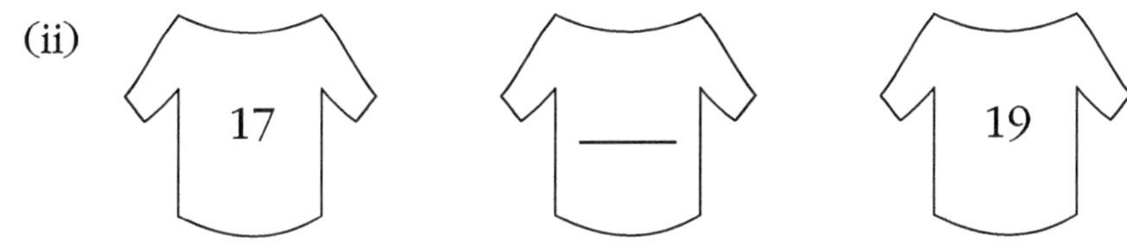

(iii)

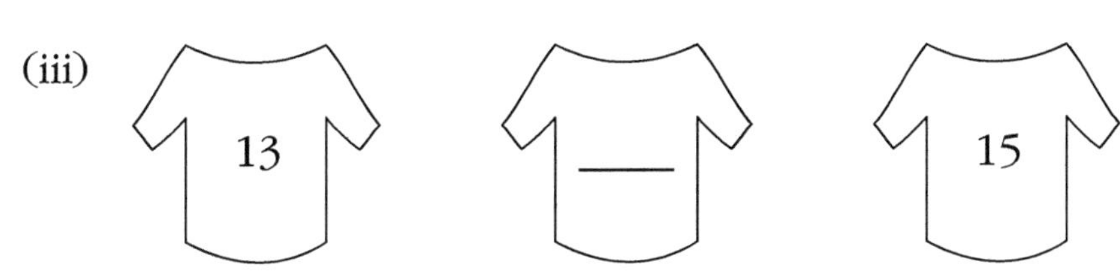

(iv)

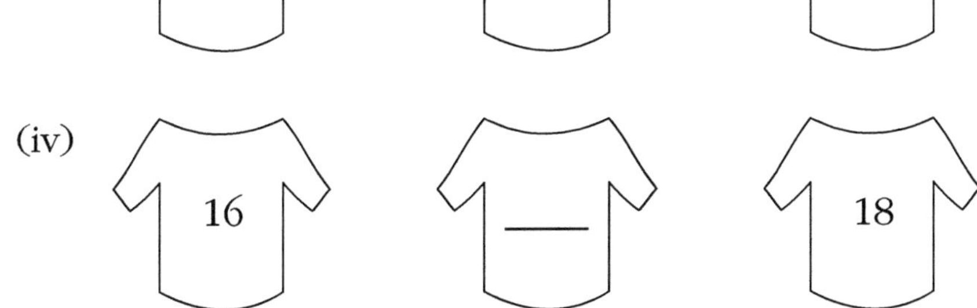

7 Circle the biggest number with red colour and smallest number with blue colour.

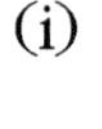

(i)

(ii)

(iii)

(iv)

(v)

(vi)

(vii)

(viii)

8 Add the following.

(i) $6+7$ = ____________ (ii) $8+6$ = ____________

(iii) $2+9$ = ____________ (iv) $12+4$ = ____________

(v) $17+2$ = ____________ (vi) $14+5$ = ____________

(vii) $18+2$ = ____________ (viii) $16+0$ = ____________

9 Solve these.

(i) 7 + 4 = ____

(ii) 12 + 7 = ____

(iii) 9 + 5 = ____

(iv) 13 + 6 = ____

(v) 15 + 2 = ____

(vi) 11 + 5 = ____

(vii) 12 + 6 = ____

(viii) 10 + 8 = ____

(ix) 16 + 1 = ____

(x) 11 + 4 = ____

10 Solve these.

(i) 18 − 3 = ____

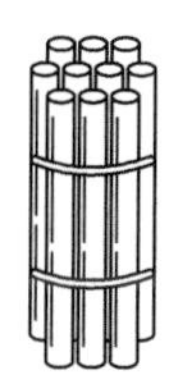
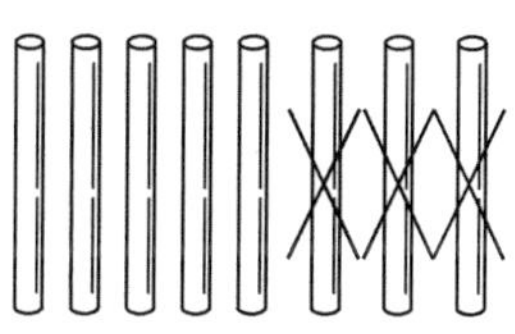

(ii) 17 − 3 = ____

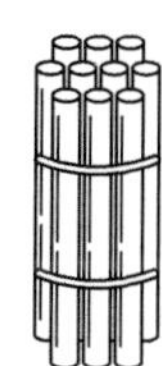
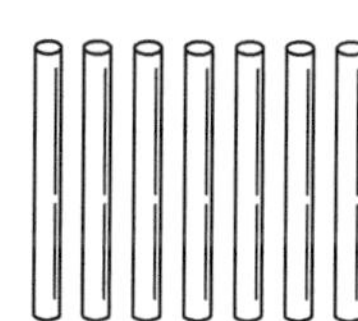

(iii) 18 − 5 = ____

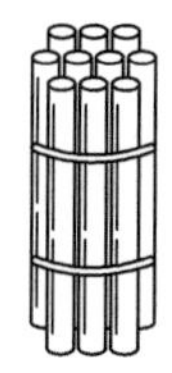
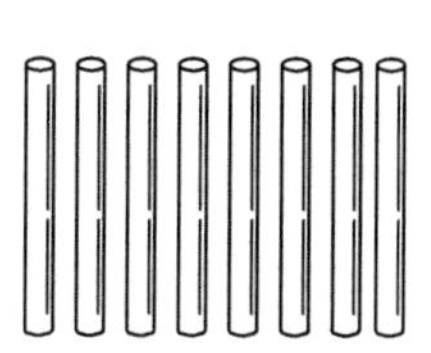

(iv) 19 − 8 = ____

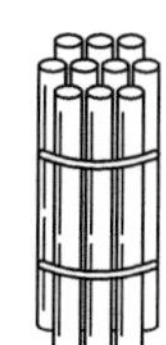
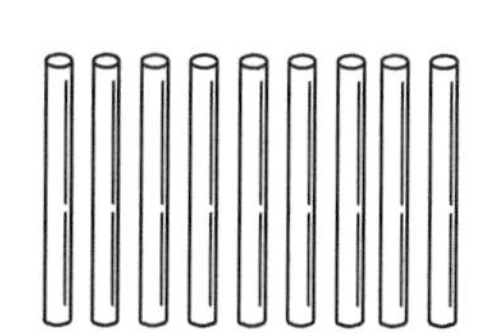

(v) 14 − 4 = ____

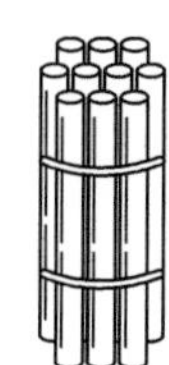
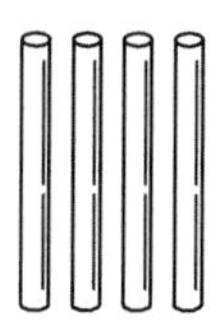

(vi) 15 − 4 = ____

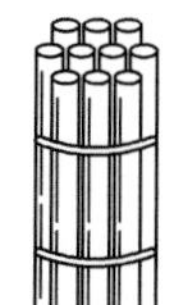
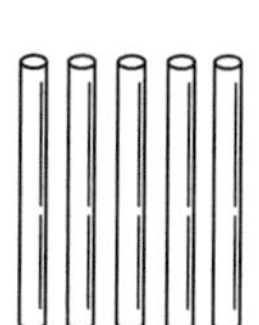

[Chapter **6**]

Time

1 Fill in the blanks.

Write M for Morning, A for Afternoon, E for Evening and N for Night.

(i) You eat dinner in the ☐

(ii) You get ready for bed in the ☐

(iii) You get out of school in the ☐

(iv) You eat breakfast in the ☐

(v) You go to school in the ☐

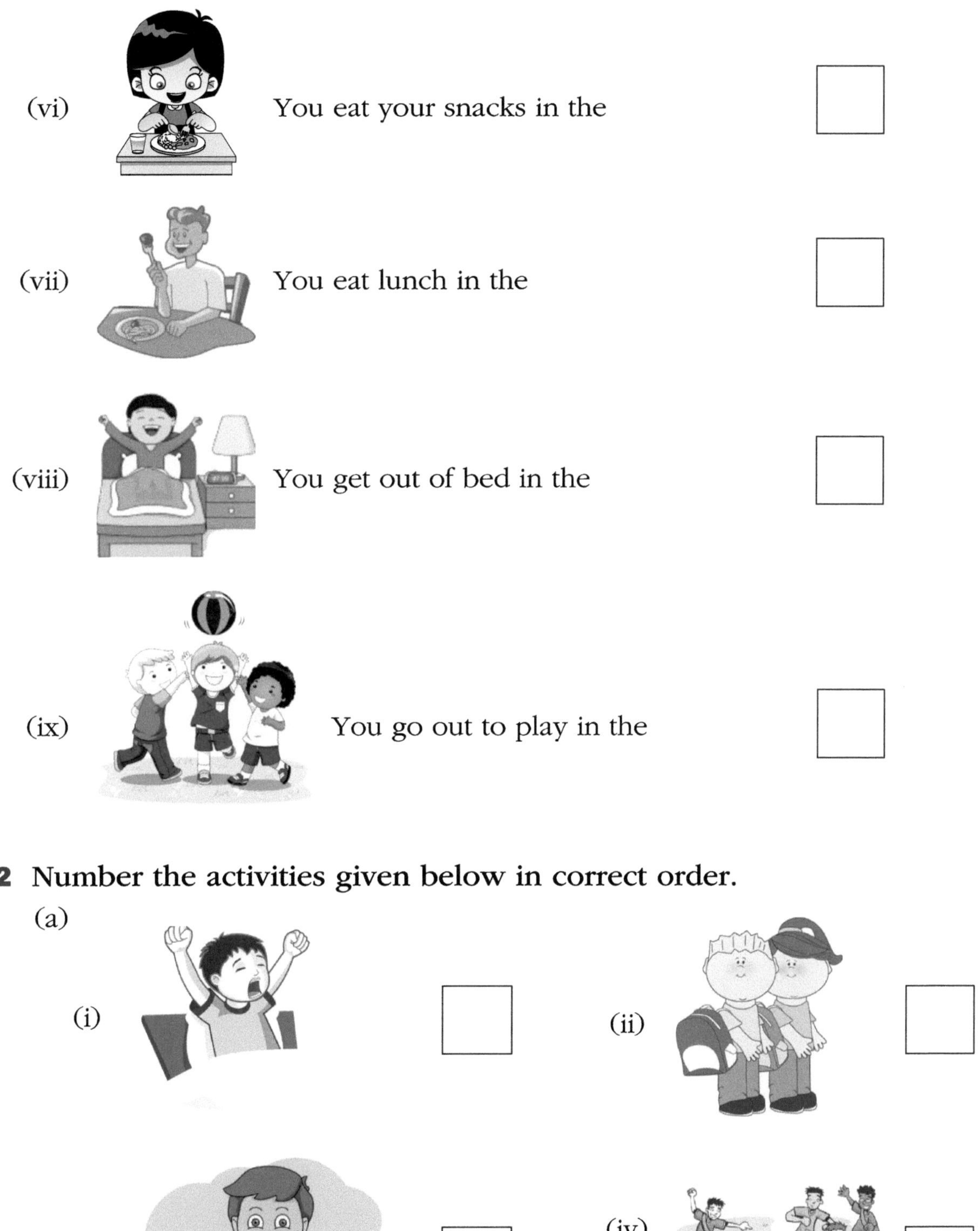

(vi) You eat your snacks in the

(vii) You eat lunch in the

(viii) You get out of bed in the

(ix) You go out to play in the

2 Number the activities given below in correct order.

(a)

(i)

(ii)

(iii)

(iv)

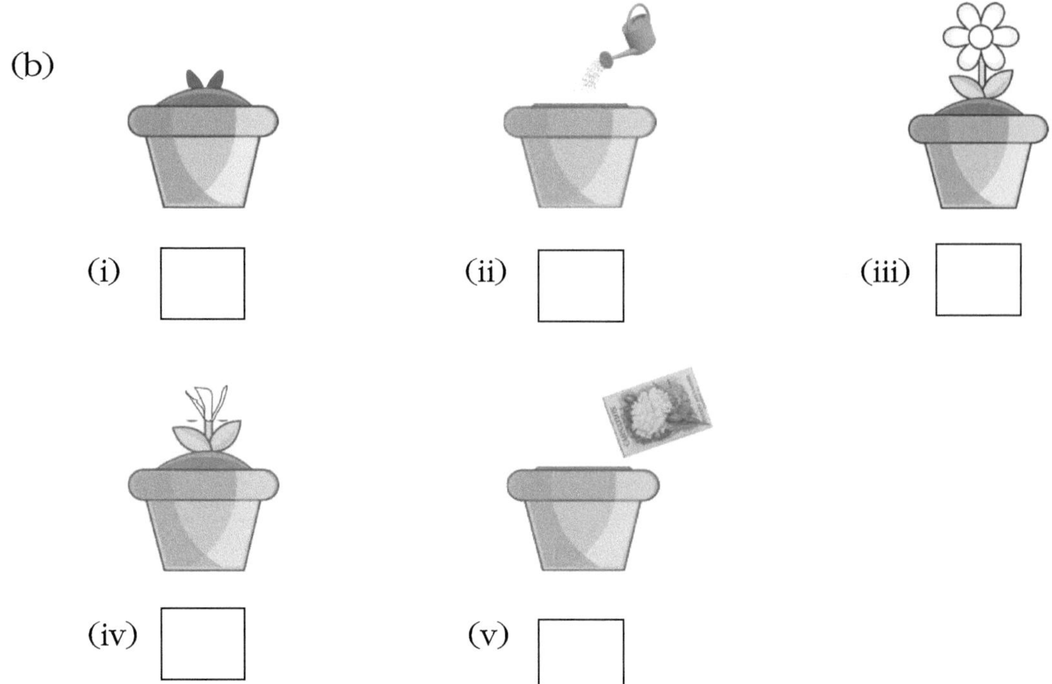

3 Tick (✓) the activity in each part that will take longer time.

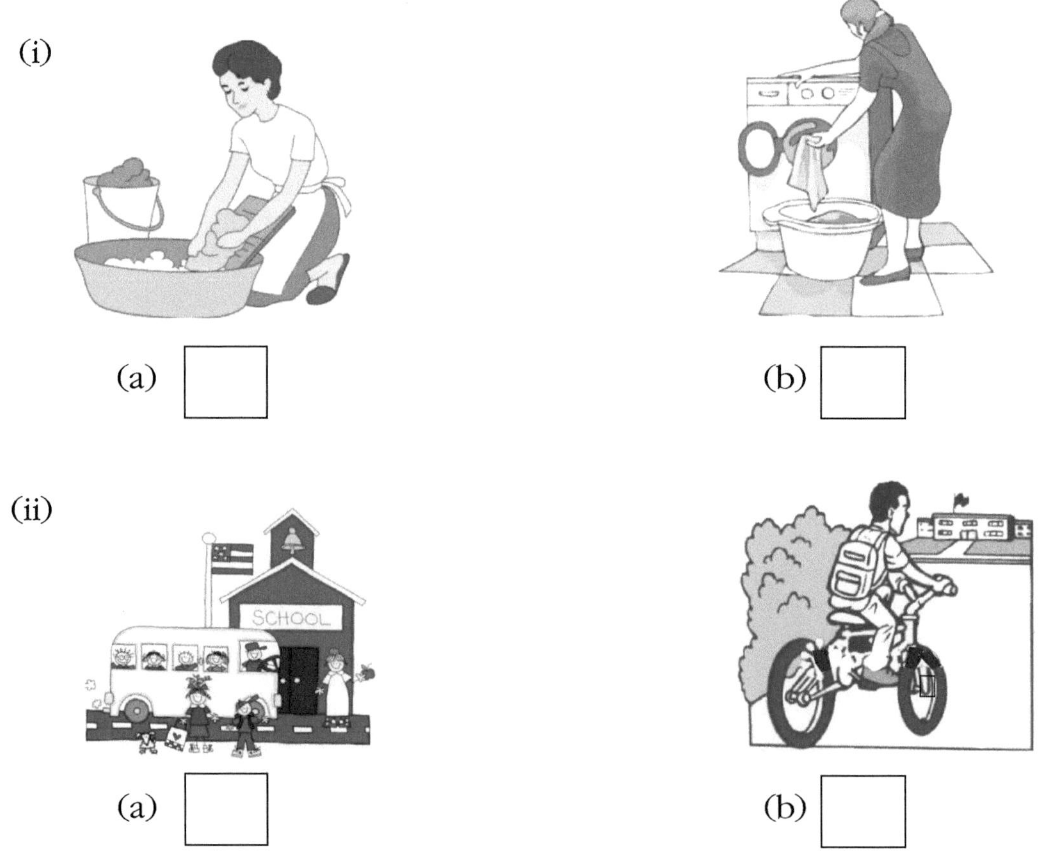

[Chapter 7]

Measurement

1 Longer and Shorter.

Tick (✓) the longer object and cross (✗) the shorter object.

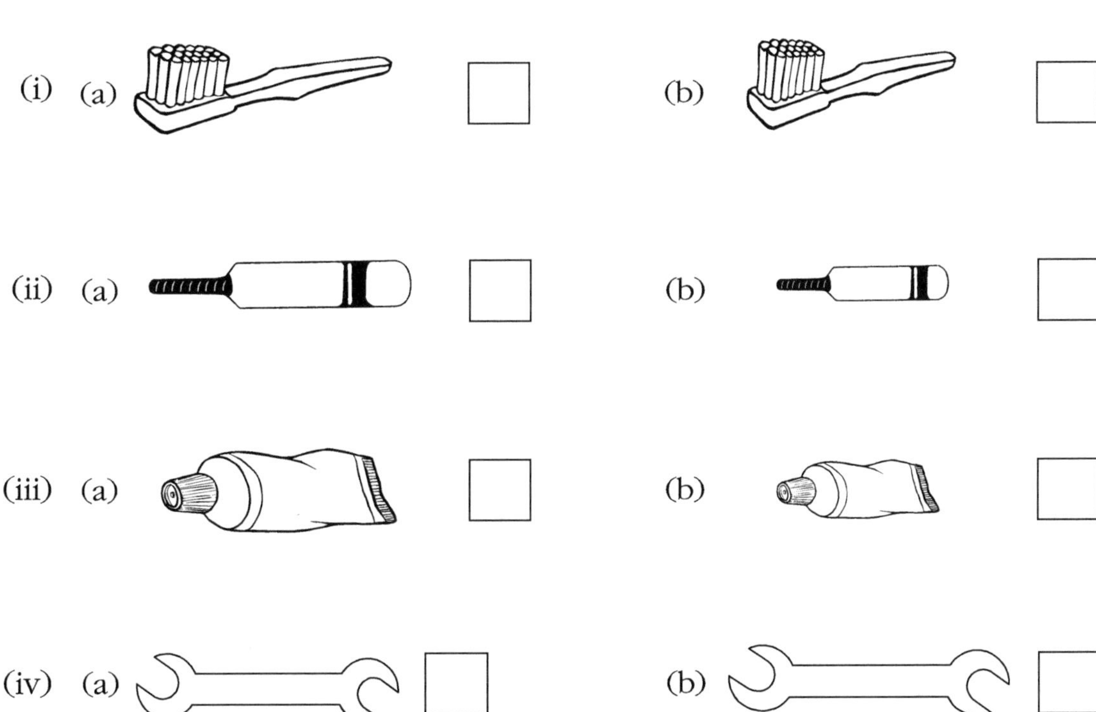

(i) (a) ☐ (b) ☐

(ii) (a) ☐ (b) ☐

(iii) (a) ☐ (b) ☐

(iv) (a) ☐ (b) ☐

(v) (a) ☐ (b) ☐

2 **Longest and Shortest.**

(i) Tick (✓) the longest car.

(a) (b) (c)

(ii) Tick (✓) the longest key.

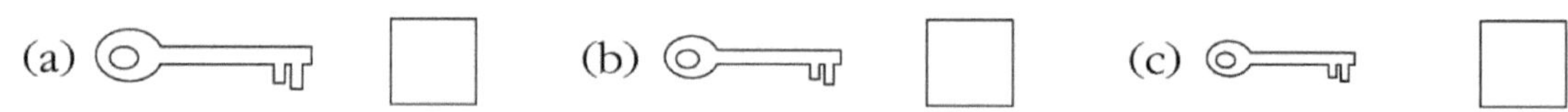

(iii) Tick (✓) the shortest pencil.

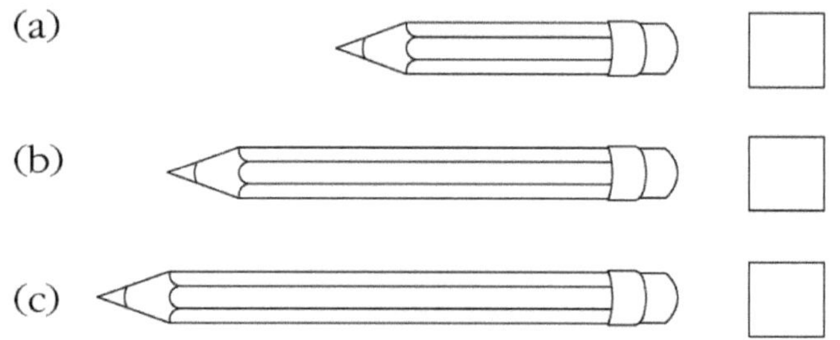

(iv) Tick (✓) the longest truck.

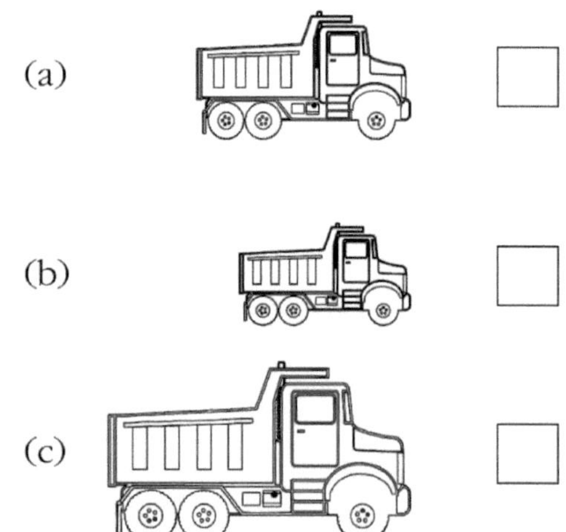

3 Taller and Shorter.

(i) Tick (✓) the taller building.

(ii) Tick (✓) the shorter table fan.

(iii) Tick (✓) the taller vase.

(iv) Tick (✓) the taller table.

(v) Tick (✓) the shorter lamp.

4 Tallest and Shortest.

(i) Tick (✓) the tallest object.

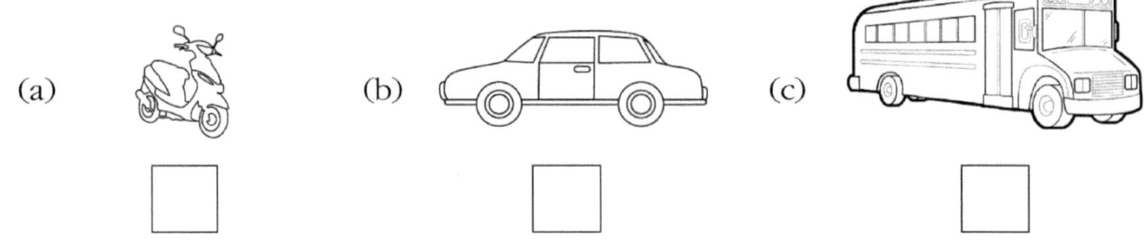

(ii) Tick (✓) the shortest table.

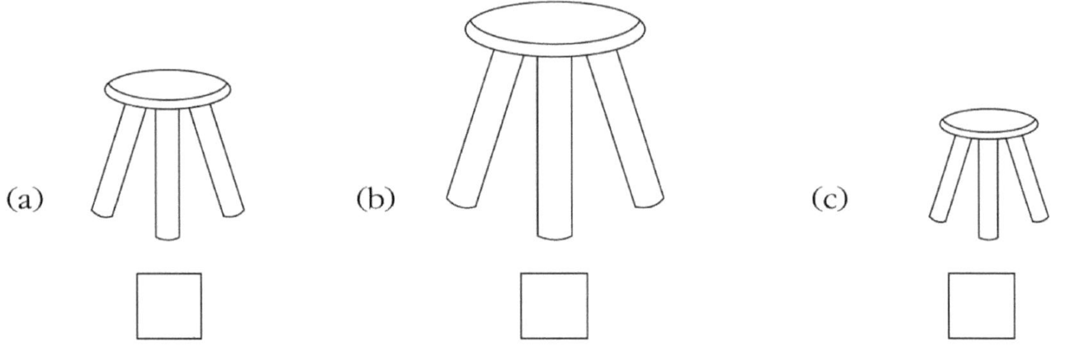

(iii) Tick (✓) the shortest animal.

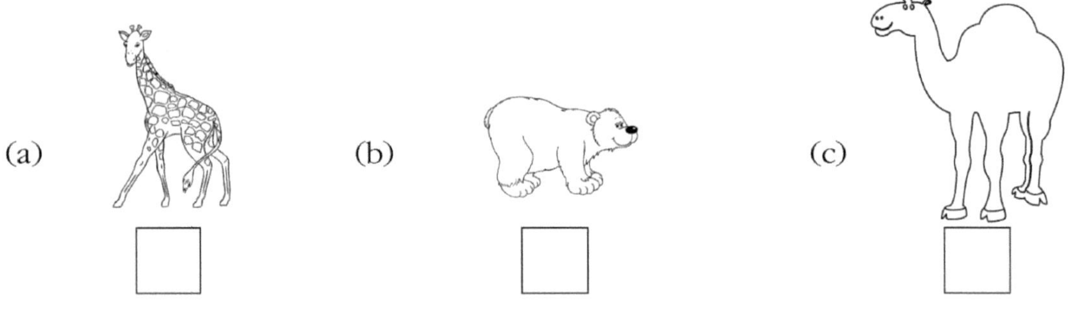

(iv) Tick (✓) the tallest person.

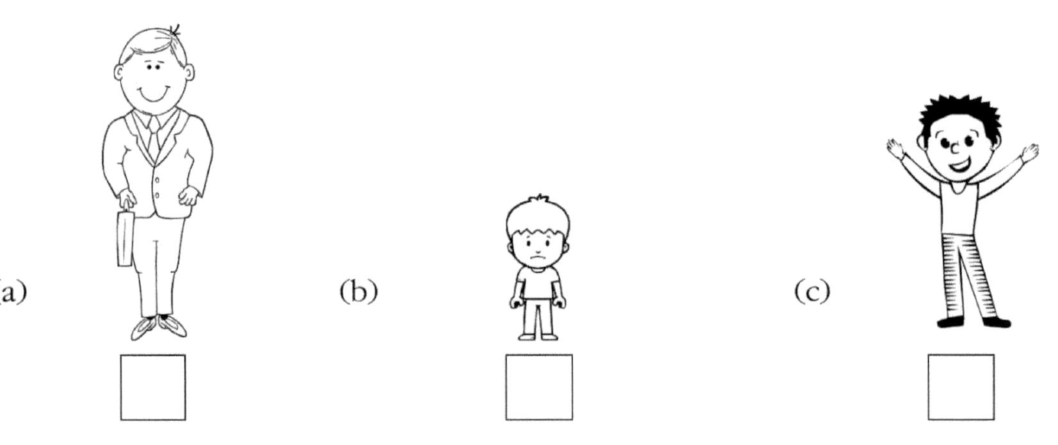

5 **Thicker and Thinner.**

(i) Tick (✓) the thicker object.

(a) (b)

(ii) Tick (✓) the thinner object.

(a) (b)

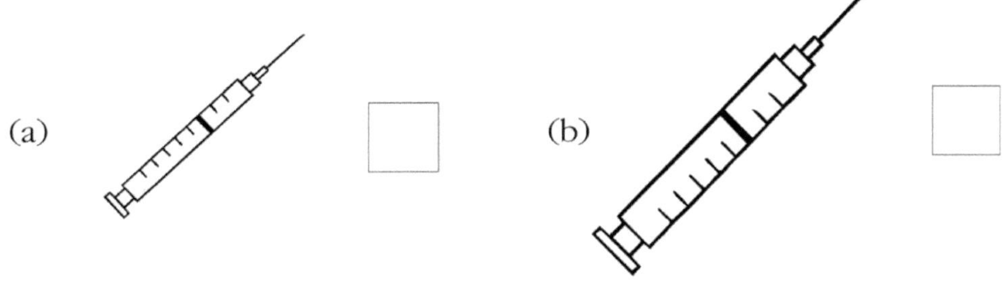

(iii) Tick (✓) the thinner object.

(a) (b)

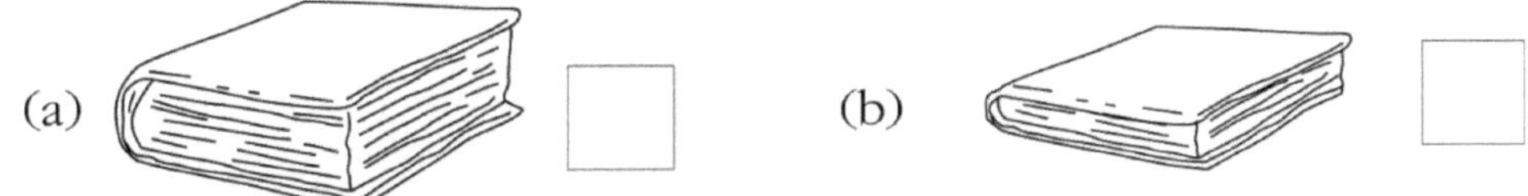

(iv) Tick (✓) the thicker object.

(a) (b)

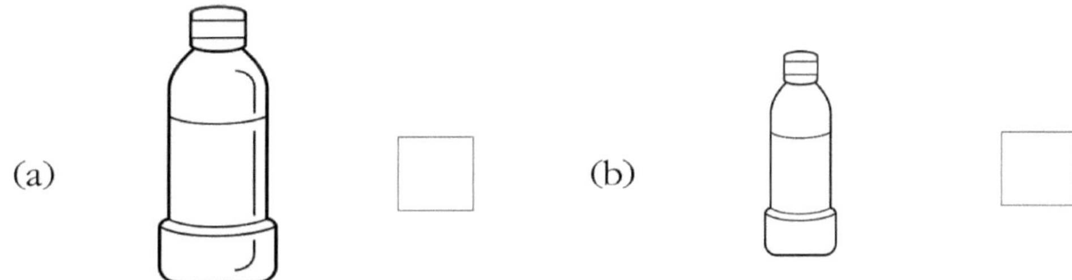

6 **Thickest and Thinnest.**

(i) Tick (✓) the thickest object.

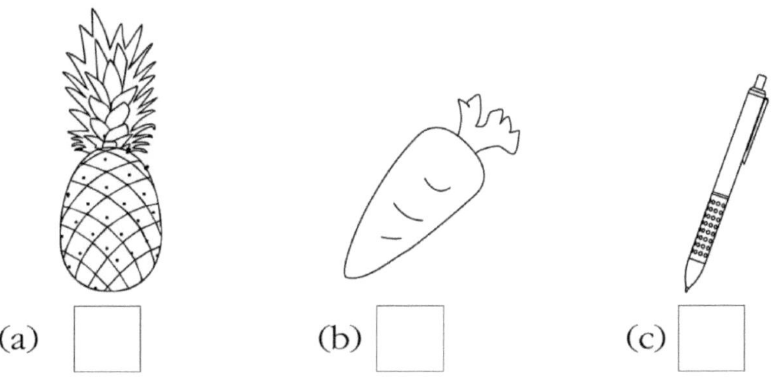

(a) (b) (c)

(ii) Tick (✓) the thinnest object.

(a) ☐ (b) ☐ (c) ☐

7 Heavier and Lighter.

(i) Tick (✓) the heavier animal.

(a) ☐ (b) ☐

(ii) Tick (✓) the heavier vehicle.

(a) ☐ (b) ☐

(iii) Tick (✓) the lighter animal.

(a) ☐ (b) ☐

(iv) Tick (✓) the lighter object.

8 Heaviest and Lightest.

(i) Tick (✓) the lightest object.

(a)

(b) 

(c) 

(ii) Tick (✓) the heaviest object.

(a) 

(b) 

(c) 

(iii) Tick (✓) the heaviest object.

(a) 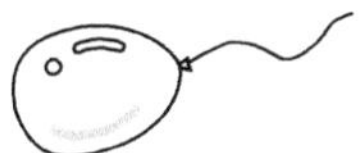

(b) 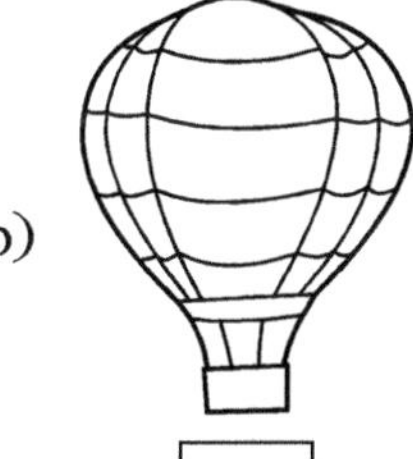

(c) 

(iv) Tick (✓) the lightest object.

(a) 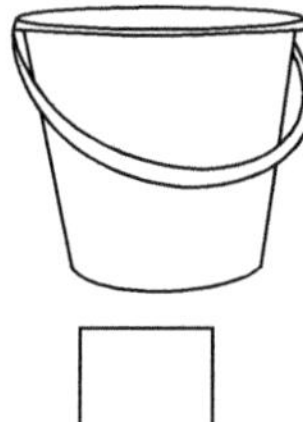

(b) 

(c) 

[Chapter 8]

Numbers from Twenty-one to Fifty

1 Write the number. One has been done for you.

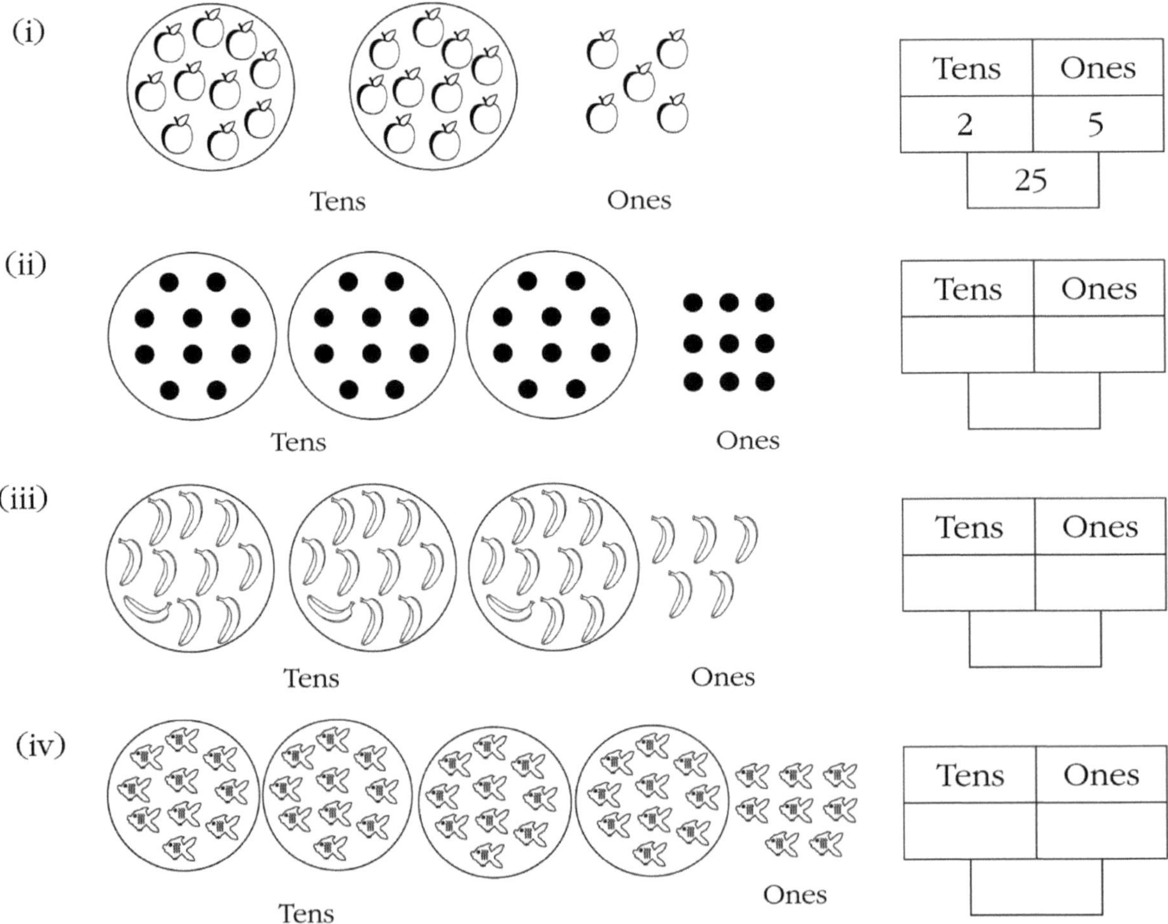

(i)

Tens	Ones
2	5

25

(ii)

Tens	Ones

(iii)

Tens	Ones

(iv)

Tens	Ones

2 Fill in the boxes. One has been done for you.

(i)

Tens	Ones
2	7

= 27

(ii)

Tens	Ones
3	0

= ☐

(iii)

Tens	Ones
3	1

= ☐

(iv)

Tens	Ones
3	9

= ☐

(v)

Tens	Ones
4	5

= ☐

(vi)

Tens	Ones
4	8

= ☐

3 Draw and fill in the boxes (numbers from 41 to 50). One has been done for you.

(i)

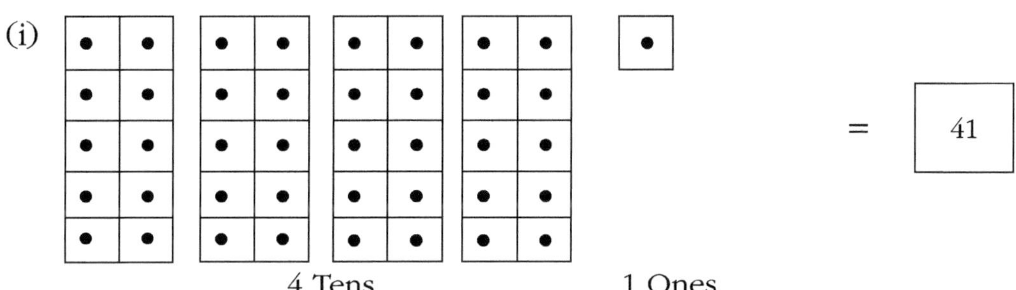

= 41

4 Tens 1 Ones

(ii)

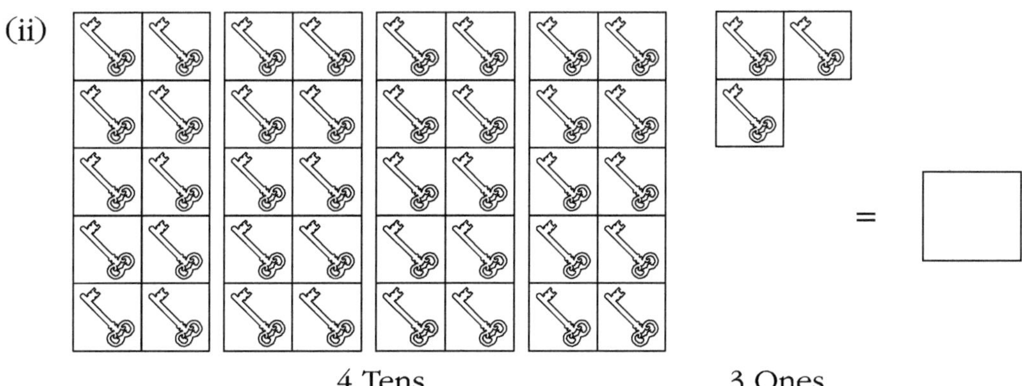

= ☐

4 Tens 3 Ones

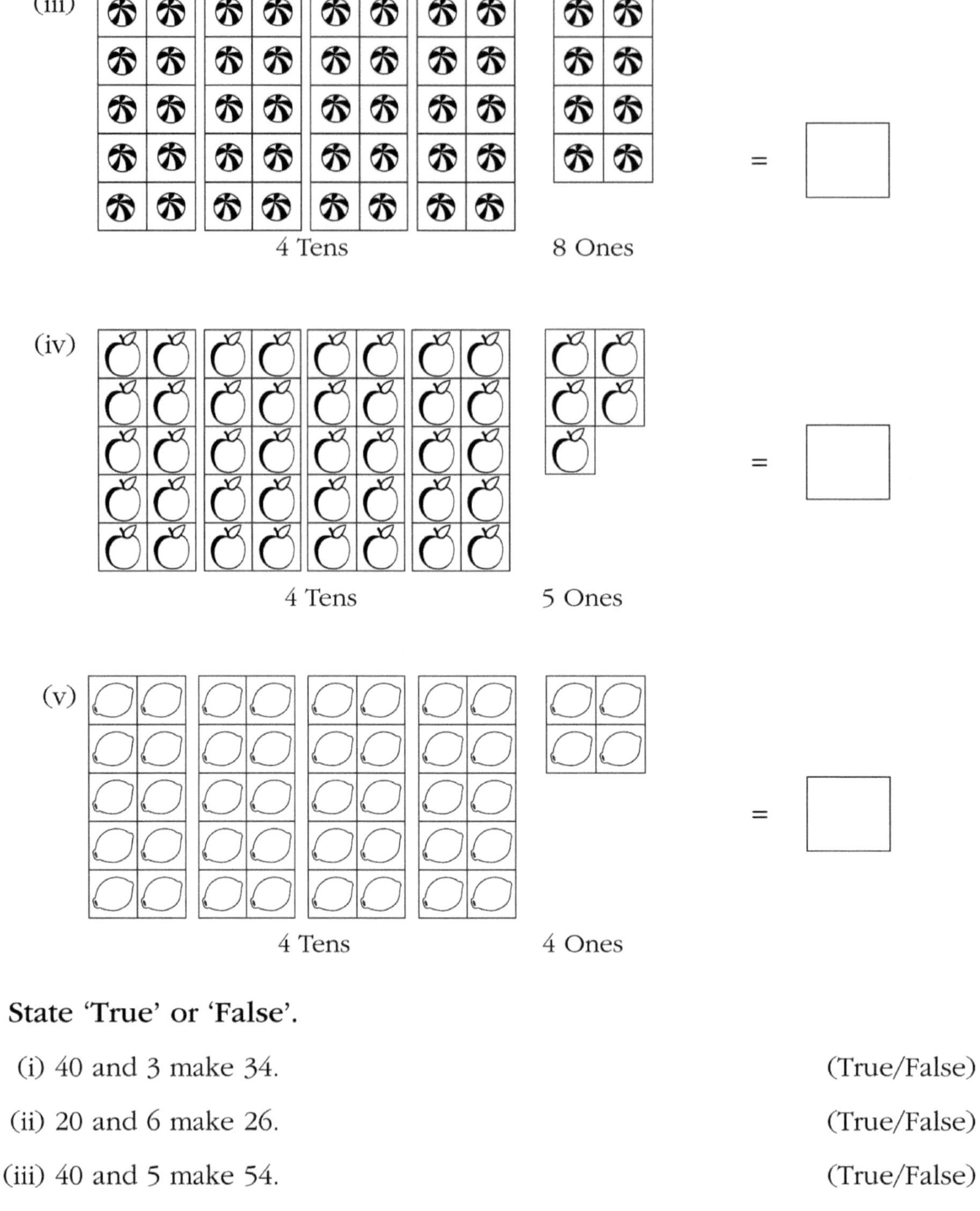

4 **State 'True' or 'False'.**

(i) 40 and 3 make 34. (True/False)

(ii) 20 and 6 make 26. (True/False)

(iii) 40 and 5 make 54. (True/False)

(iv) 20 and 9 make 29. (True/False)

(v) 30 and 7 make 47. (True/False)

[Chapter **9**]

Data Handling

1 Look at the picture given below.

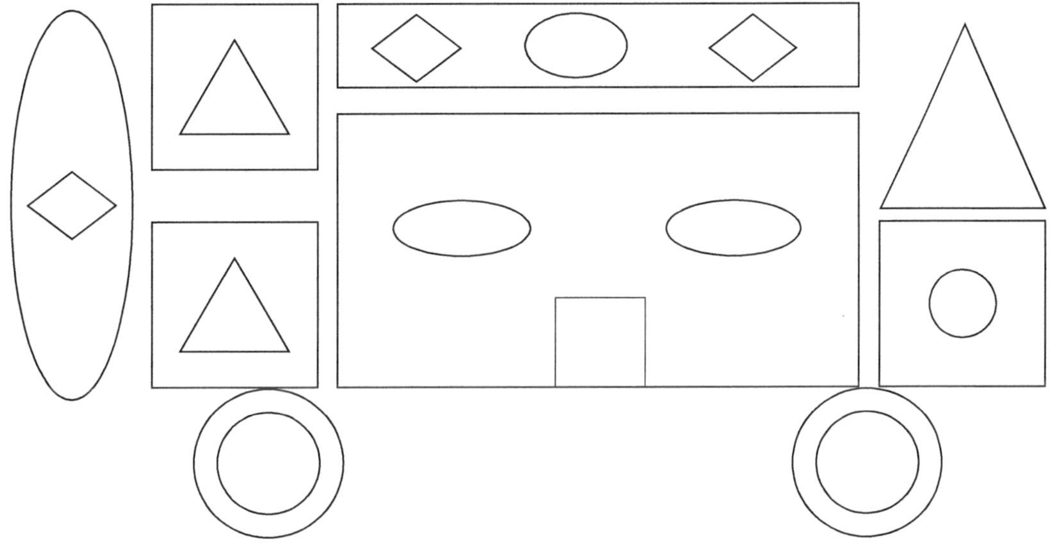

Count the shapes in the above picture.

(i) =

(ii) =

(iii) =

(iv) =

(v) =

(vi) =

2 Look at the picture given below.

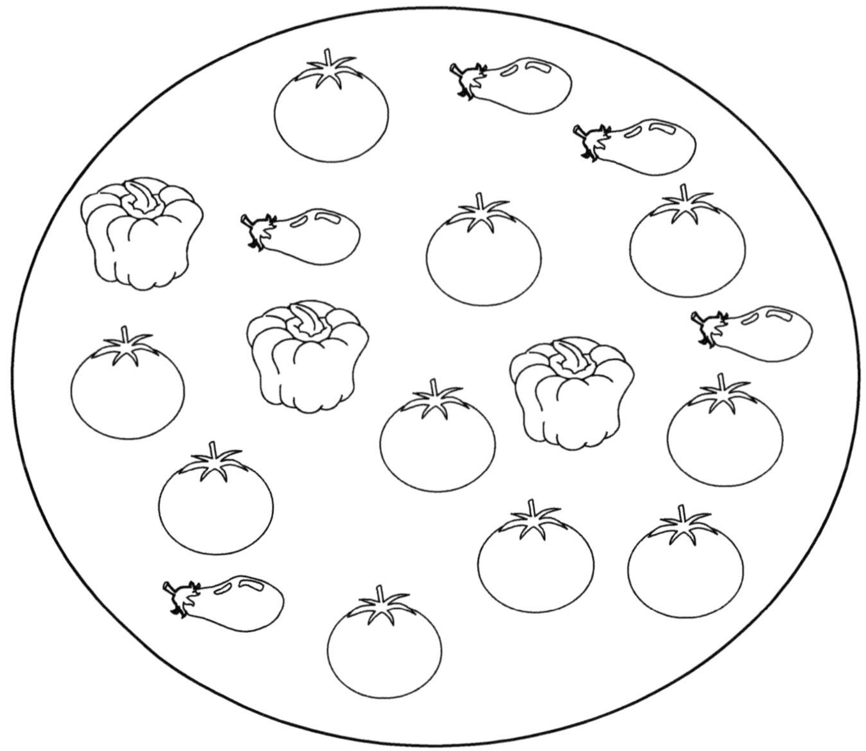

State 'True' or 'False' on the basis of above picture.

(i) Number of [tomato] = 12 ☐

(ii) Number of [brinjal] = 5 ☐

(iii) Number of [capsicum] = 3 ☐

3 **Given below are the names of vegetables.**

(i) Count the number of letters in each name (word). One has been done for you.

	Name	Number of letters
(a)	T O M A T O	6
(b)	B R I N J A L	
(c)	O N I O N	
(d)	C A R R O T	
(e)	C A B B A G E	
(f)	C U C U M B E R	

(ii) How many names have six letters? ☐

(iii) How many names have five letters? ☐

(iv) How many names have seven letters? ☐

(v) How many times (A) comes in all the names together? ☐

(vi) How many times (O) comes in all the names together? ☐

(vii) How many times (I) comes in all the names together? ☐

[Chapter **10**]

Patterns

1 Extend the sequence in the same pattern that follows.

(i)

(ii)

(iii)

(iv)

(v)

2 Complete the pattern.

(i)

(ii)

(iii)

(iv)

3 Fill in the boxes to complete the sequence.

4 Study the pattern and fill in the missing numbers.

(i)

(ii)

(iii)

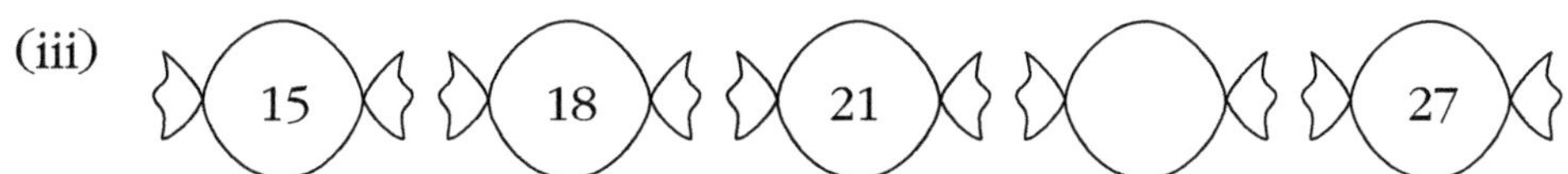

(iv)

24 23 22 19

5 Complete the pattern.

(i)

(ii)

(iii)

(iv)

6 Choose the correct pattern that comes next.

(i) (a) (b) (c)

(ii) (a) (b) (c)

(iii) (a) (b) (c)

(iv) (a) (b) (c)

[Chapter 11]

Numbers

1 Draw the circles as per the given numbers. One has been done for you.

(i)

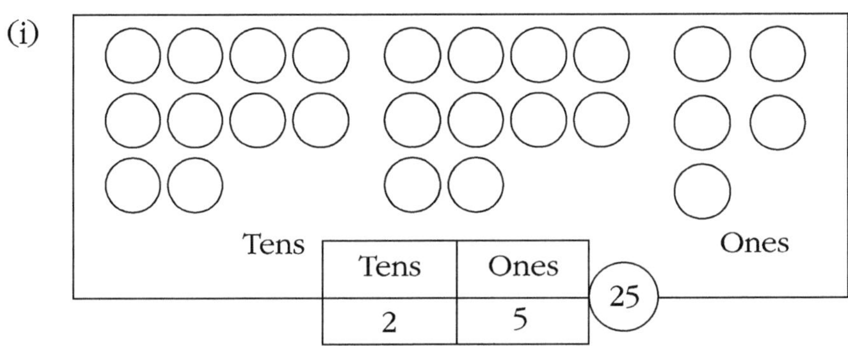

(ii)

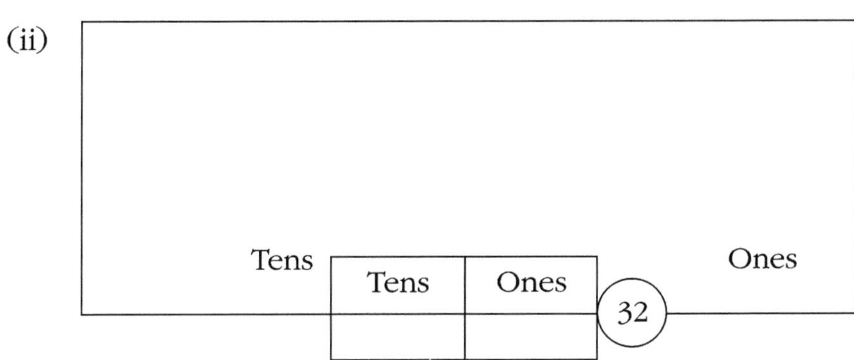

(iii)

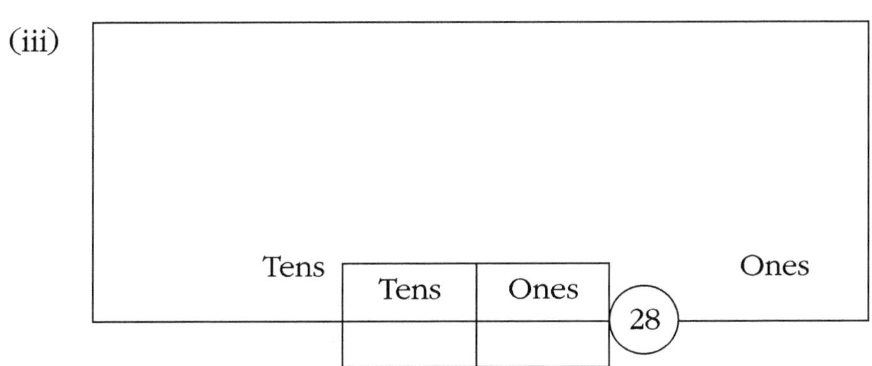

2 Write the number in the given space. One has been done for you.

(i)

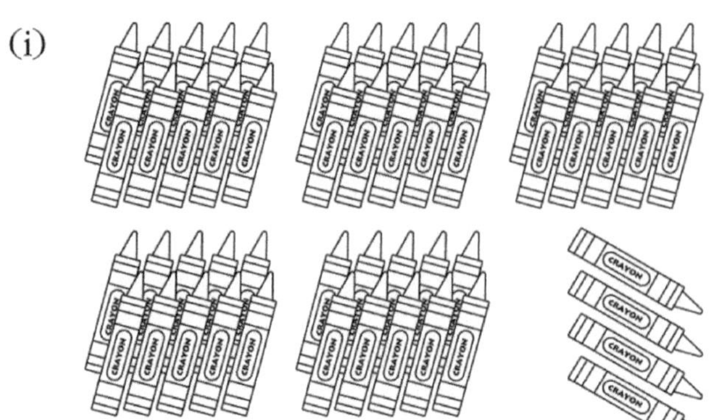

Tens	Ones
5	4

54

(ii)

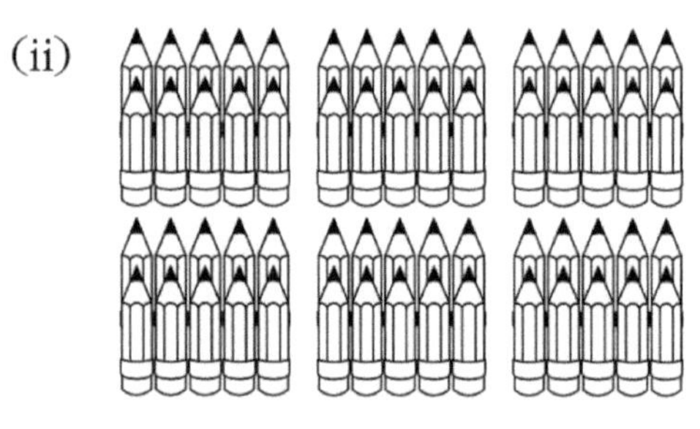

Tens	Ones

(iii)

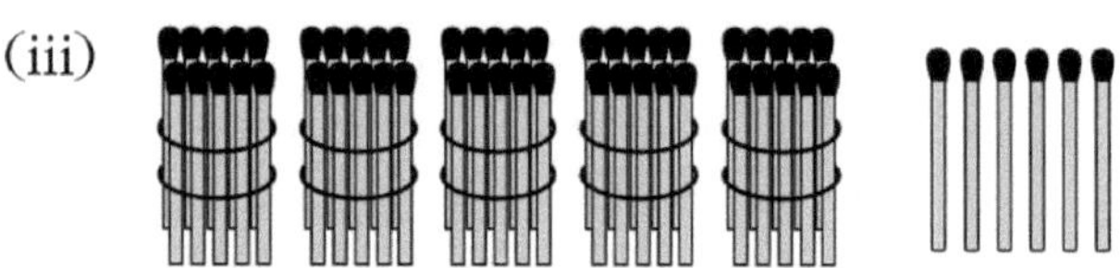

Tens	Ones

(iv)

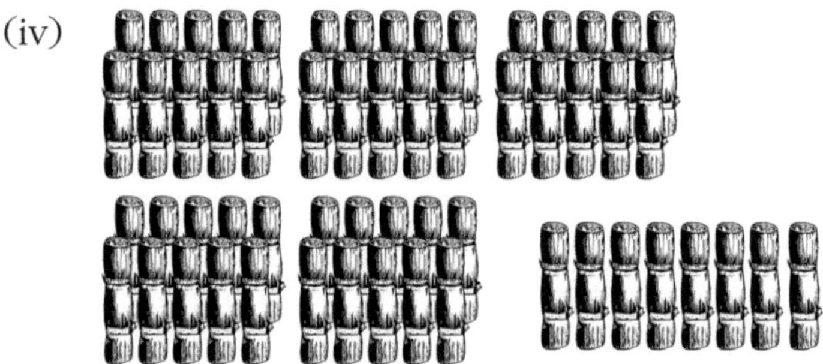

Tens	Ones

(v)

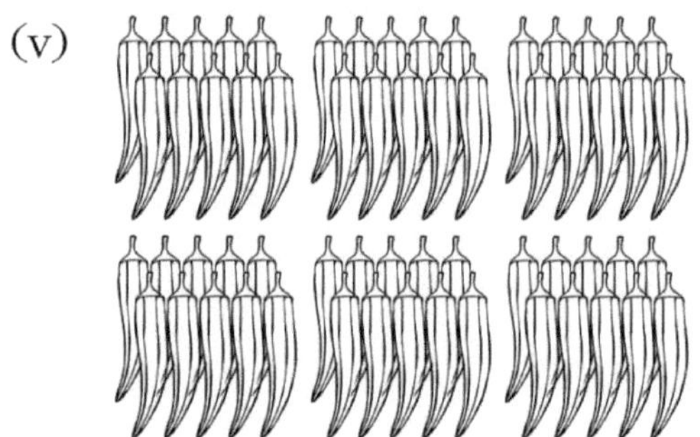

Tens	Ones

3 Fill in the boxes. One has been done for you.

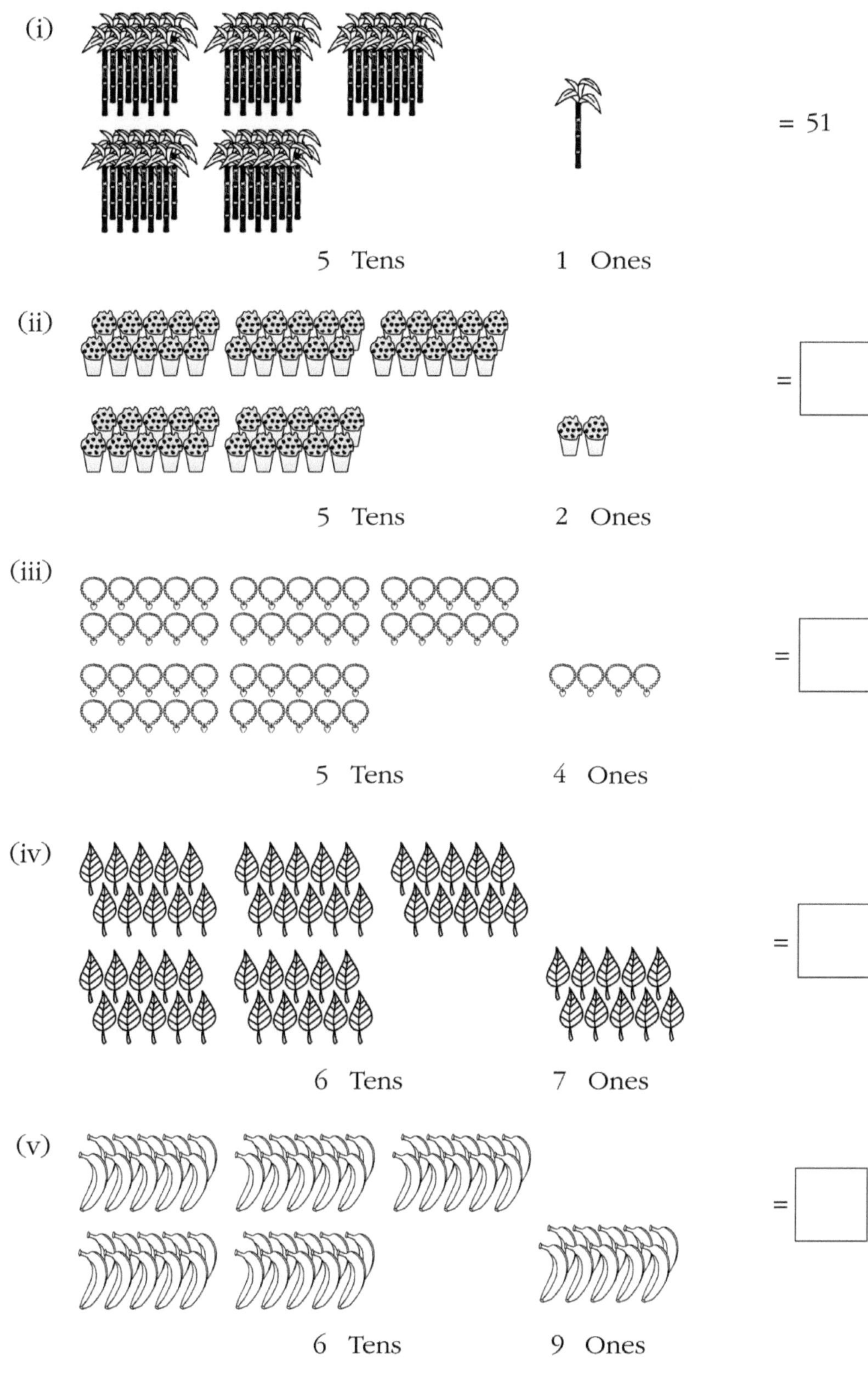

4 Write the following numerals as tens and ones. One has been done for you.

(i)	64	=	6	tens	4	ones
(ii)	76	=		tens		ones
(iii)	51	=		tens		ones
(iv)	82	=		tens		ones
(v)	96	=		tens		ones
(vi)	59	=		tens		ones
(vii)	65	=		tens		ones
(viii)	84	=		tens		ones
(ix)	75	=		tens		ones
(x)	66	=		tens		ones

5 Complete the sequence by filling the missing numbers.

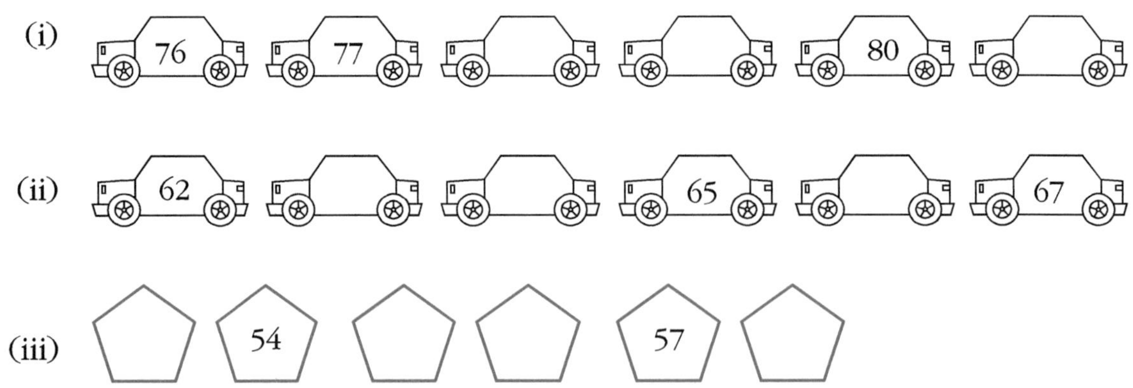

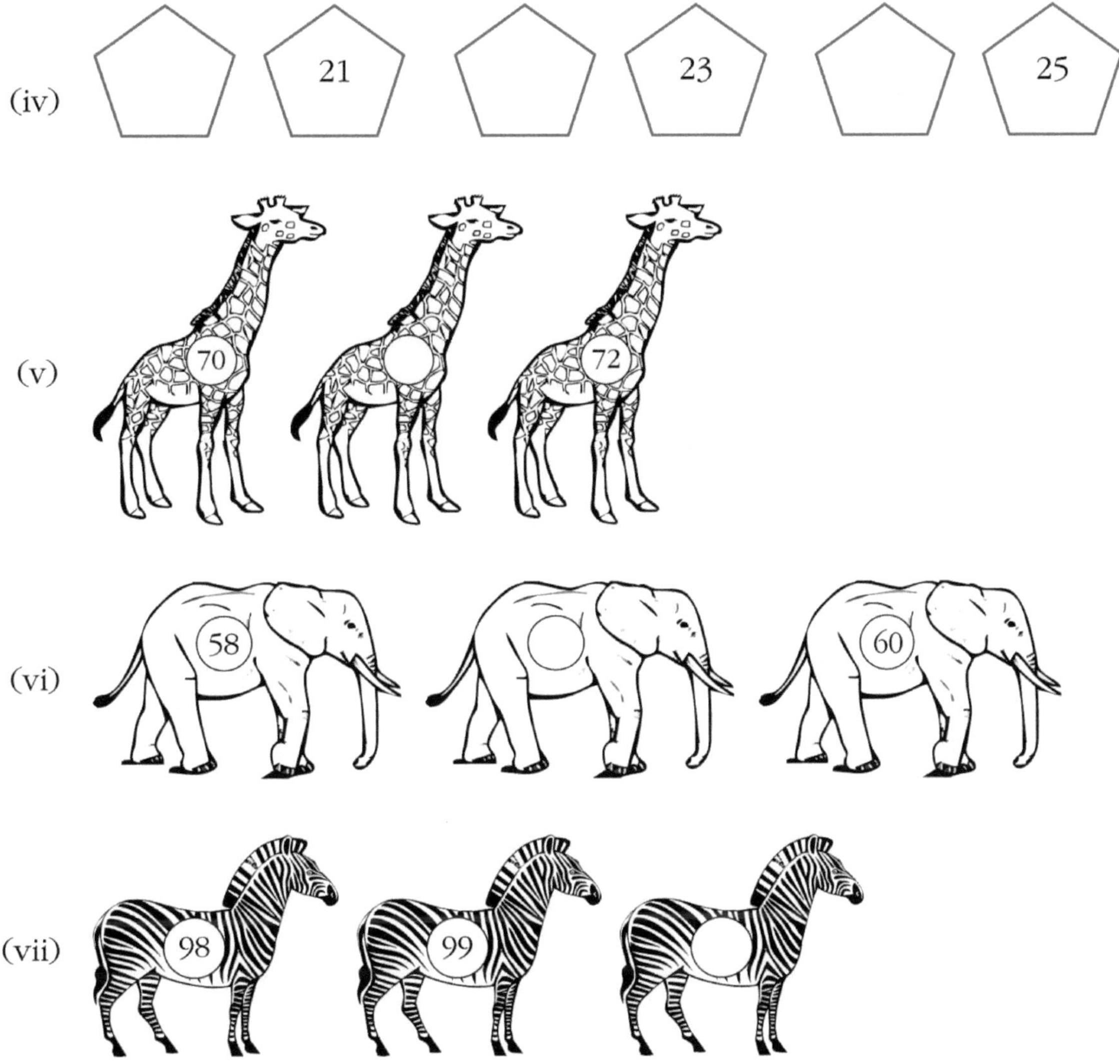
(iv)
21
23
25
(v)
70
72
(vi)
58
60
(vii)
98
99

Chapter 12

Money

1 Match the rupees and coins with correct values. One has been done for you.

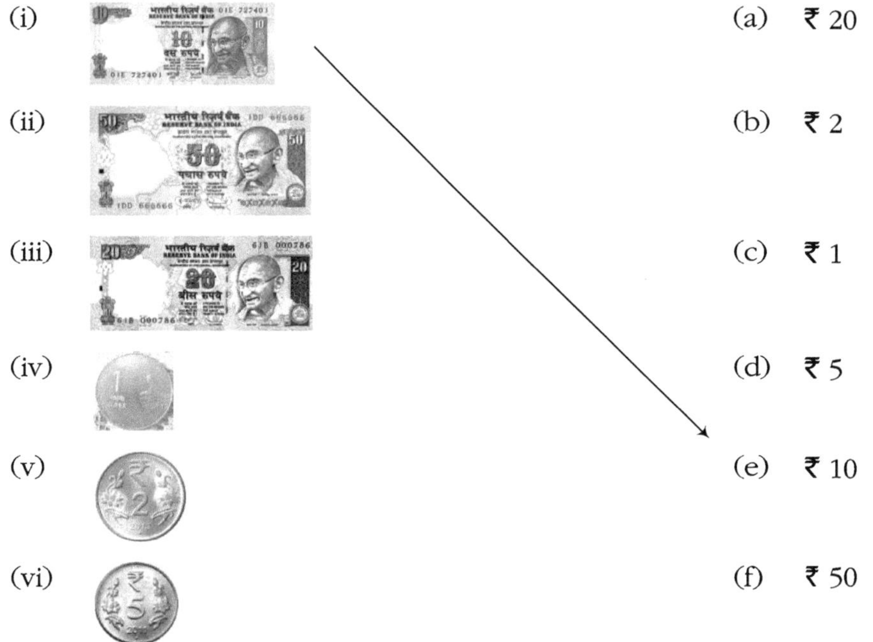

2 (i) Make the given amount using different possible combinations of coins.

1 rupee

2 rupee

2 rupee

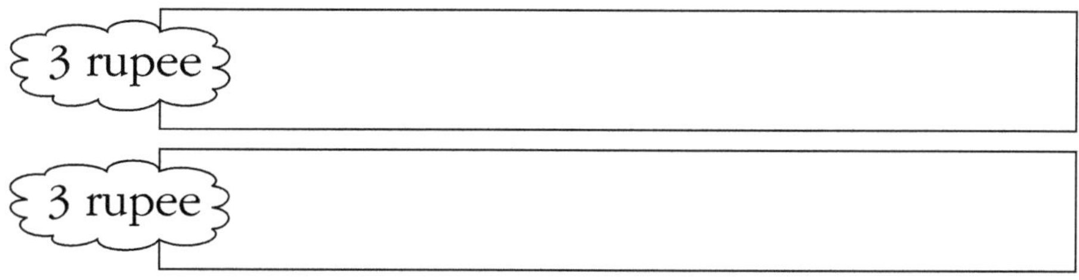

(ii) Make the given amount using different possible combination of coins.

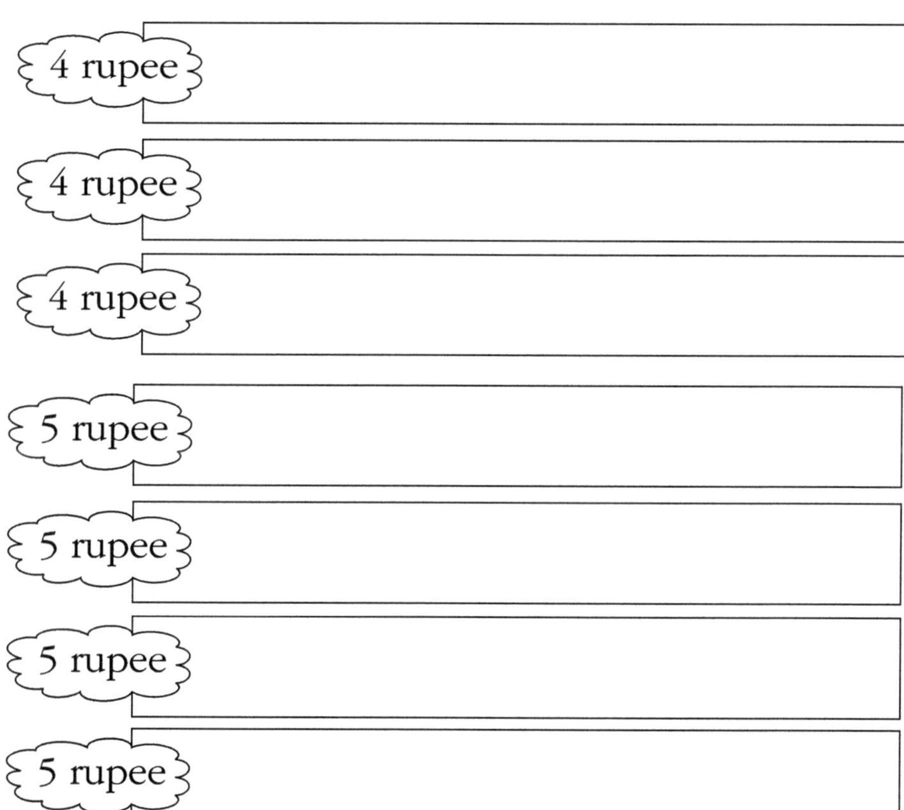

6 rupee

6 rupee

6 rupee

6 rupee

3 Count and write the total amount of money. One has been done for you.

(i)  = ₹ 18

(ii)  = 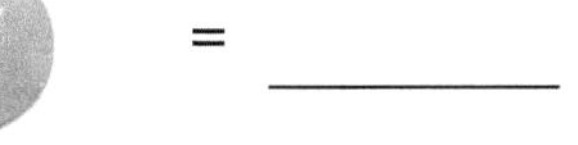 ________

(iii) = ________

(iv)  = ________

4 Count the total amount of money and mark (✓), if you can buy the object and mark (✗), if you can't buy the object.

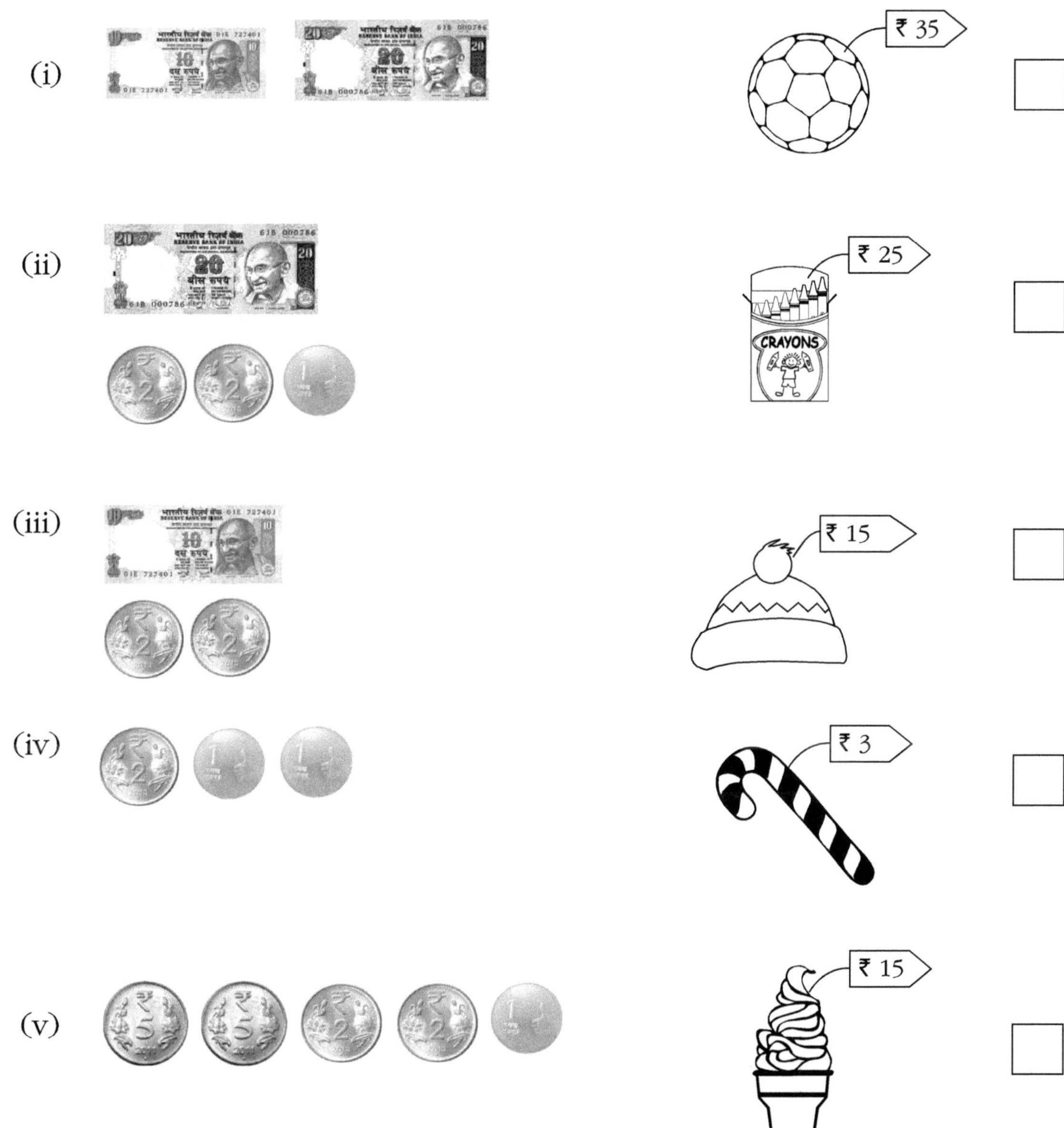

5 Guess and match the items with the correct amount. One has been done for you.

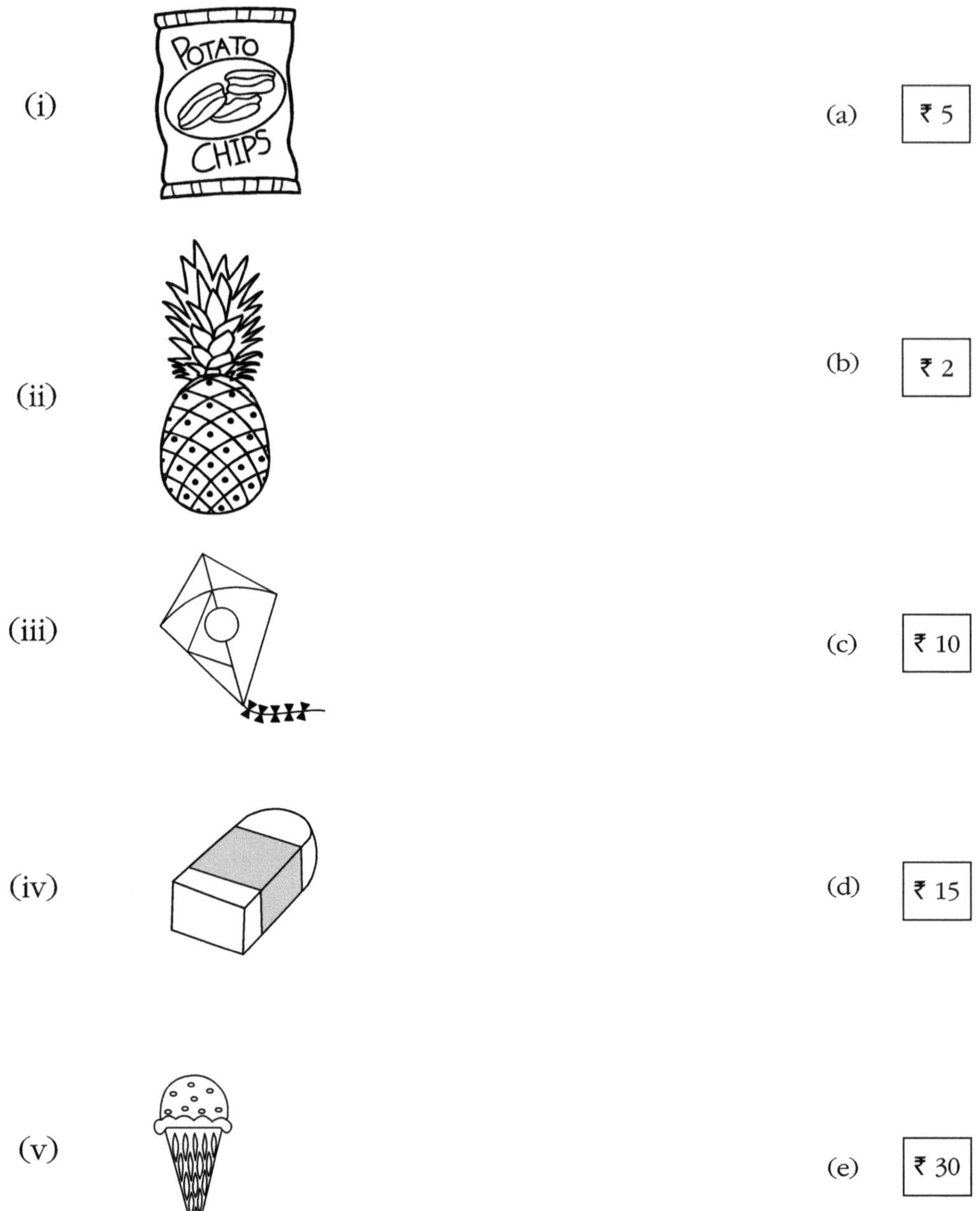

Chapter 13

How Many

1 Write the number of objects.

(i)  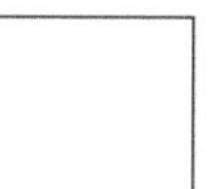

(ii) 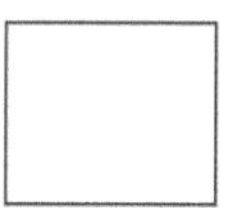

(iii)  

(iv) 

(v) 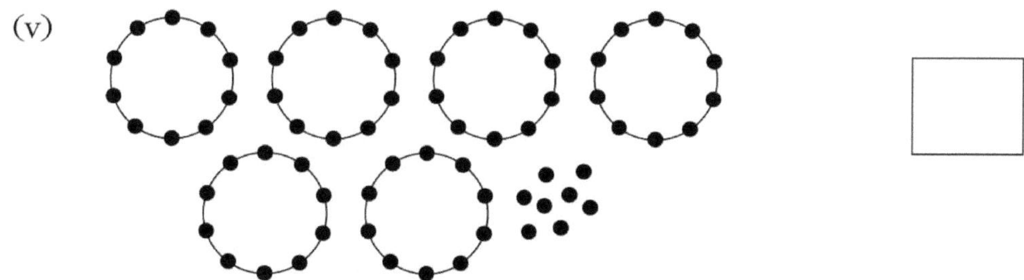

(vi)

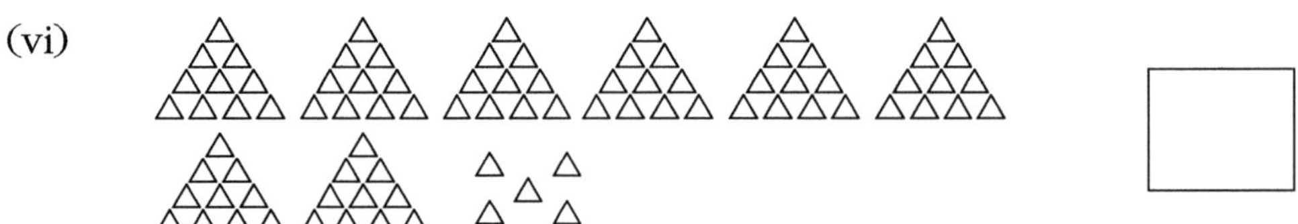

2 How much will the following cost?

(i)

(ii)

(iii)

(iv)

3 Write the number name.

	Number	Number name
(i)	16	
(ii)	23	
(iii)	19	

	Number	Number name
(iv)	29	
(v)	36	
(vi)	31	

4 How many tens and ones? One has been done for you.

(i) 23 = [2] tens [3] ones

(ii) 46 = [ ] tens [ ] ones

(iii) 75 = [ ] tens [ ] ones

(iv) 24 = [ ] tens [ ] ones

(v) 39 = [ ] tens [ ] ones

(vi) 62 = [ ] tens [ ] ones

(vii) 81 = [ ] tens [ ] ones

(viii) 96 = [ ] tens [ ] ones

(ix) 43 = [ ] tens [ ] ones

(x) 51 = [ ] tens [ ] ones

5 Circle the bigger number and cross out the smaller number.

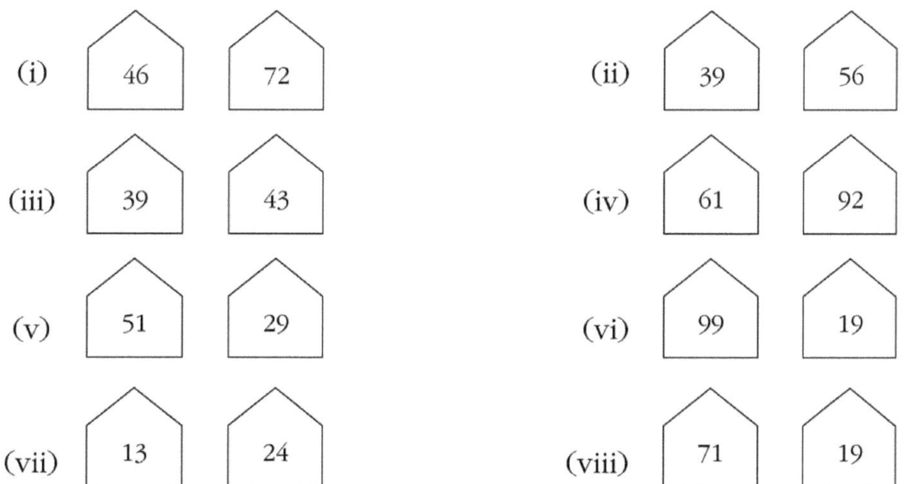

Answers

Chapter 1 Shapes and Space

3. (i) (a) ✓ (b) ✗ (ii) (a) ✓ (c) ✗
(iii) (c) ✓ (a) ✗ (iv) (a) ✓ (c) ✗

6. (i) (a) (ii) (a) (iii) (c) (iv) (a)

7. (i) above (ii) on
(iii) on (iv) above
(v) above (vi) on

8. (i) (c) ✓ (b) ✗ (ii) (c) ✓ (a) ✗
(iii) (a) ✓ (b) ✗ (iv) (b) ✓ (c) ✗

10. (i)–(b), (ii)–(c), (iii)–(a), (iv)–(e),
(v)–(d)

Chapter 2 Numbers from One to Nine

2. (i) 1 (ii) 5 (iii) 2 (iv) 7
(v) 6 (vi) 3 (vii) 9 (viii) 4

3. (i) (a) ✗ (b) ✓ (ii) (a) ✗ (b) ✓
(iii) (a) ✓ (b) ✗ (iv) (a) ✗ (b) ✓
(v) (a) ✓ (b) ✗

4. (i)–(c), (ii)–(d), (iii)–(b),
(iv)–(e), (v)–(a)

6. (i)–(d), (ii)–(e), (iii)–(f), (iv)–(g),
(v)–(c), (vi)–(h), (vii)–(b), (viii)–(a)

8. (i) 9 (ii) 5 (iii) 4 (iv) 7

9. (i) 4 (ii) 8 (iii) 6 (iv) 5
(v) 3 (vi) 7

10. (i) 2 (ii) 9 (iii) 4 (iv) 3
(v) 7 (vi) 5 (vii) 8 (viii) 7
(ix) 6 (x) 2

11. (i) (a) 4 (b) 3 (c) 2 (d) 0
(ii) (a) 3 (b) 0 (c) 1 (d) 2
(iii) (a) 5 (b) 3 (c) 1 (d) 0

Chapter 3 Addition

1. (ii) 7 (iii) 5 (iv) 6 (v) 8
(vi) 6

2. (ii) 6, 2; 8 (iii) 2, 2; 4 (iv) 2, 3; 5
(v) 4, 3; 7 (vi) 3, 2; 5

3. (i) 4, 2; 6 (ii) 4, 5; 9 (iii) 6, 1; 7
(iv) 4, 4; 8 (v) 3, 2; 5 (vi) 4, 6; 10
(vii) 2, 1; 3 (viii) 2, 2; 4

4. (ii)–(a), (iii)–(b), (iv)–(e), (v)–(d)

5. (ii) 3 (iii) 5 (iv) 9 (v) 8

6. (ii)–V–(a), (iii)–I–(e),
(iv)–VI–(d), (v)–II–(b),
(vi)–III–(f)

7. (i) 7 (ii) 8 (iii) 6 (iv) 8
(v) 4 (vi) 9 (vii) 9 (viii) 9
(ix) 8 (x) 5 (xi) 9 (xii) 7

10. (i) 8 (ii) 7 (iii) 8

Chapter 4 Subtraction

1. (ii) 8, 3, 5; 8, 3, 5 (iii) 6, 2, 4; 6, 2, 4
(iv) 6, 3, 3; 6, 3, 3 (v) 9, 2, 7; 9, 2, 7

2. (ii) 8, 2; 6 (iii) 8, 4; 4
(iv) 8, 1; 7 (v) 6, 3; 3

3. (ii) 0 (iii) 1 (iv) 2 (v) 3
(vi) 7 (vii) 9 (viii) 4 (ix) 8
(x) 5

4. (i) 5 (ii) 4 (iii) 2 (iv) 3

5. (i) 4 (ii) 9 (iii) 4 (iv) 8
(v) 0 (vi) 3 (vii) 2 (viii) 5
(ix) 8

7. (i) 5 (ii) 4
(iii) 5 (iv) 3
(v) 3

Chapter 5 Numbers from Ten to Twenty

2. (ii) 13 (iii) 15 (iv) 11 (v) 14
(vi) 17 (vii) 19

3. (ii) 18 (iii) 14 (iv) 17 (v) 20

5. (i) 13, 15 (ii) 16, 18 (iii) 11, 13 (iv) 14, 16
(v) 17, 19 (vi) 10, 12

6. (i) 16 (ii) 18
(iii) 14 (iv) 17

8. (i) 13 (ii) 14 (iii) 11 (iv) 16
(v) 19 (vi) 19 (vii) 20 (viii) 16

9. (i) 11 (ii) 19 (iii) 14 (iv) 19
(v) 17 (vi) 16 (vii) 18 (viii) 18
(ix) 17 (x) 15

10. (i) 15 (ii) 14 (iii) 13 (iv) 11
(v) 10 (vi) 11

Chapter 6 Time

1. (i) N (ii) N (iii) A (iv) M
(v) M (vi) E (vii) A (viii) M
(ix) E

2. (a) (i) 1 (ii) 3 (iii) 2 (iv) 4
(b) (i) 3 (ii) 2 (iii) 5 (iv) 4
(v) 1

3. (i) (a) (ii) (b)

Chapter 7 Measurement

1. (i) (a) ✓ (b) ✗ (ii) (a) ✓ (b) ✗
(iii) (a) ✓ (b) ✗ (iv) (a) ✗ (b) ✓
(v) (a) ✗ (b) ✓

2. (i) (a) (ii) (a) (iii) (a) (iv) (c)

3. (i) (b) (ii) (a) (iii) (b) (iv) (a)
(v) (a)

4. (i) (c) (ii) (c) (iii) (b) (iv) (a)

5. (i) (b) (ii) (a)
(iii) (b) (iv) (a)

6. (i) (a) (ii) (b)

7. (i) (a) (ii) (b)
(iii) (a) (iv) (b)

8. (i) (a) (ii) (a)
(iii) (b) (iv) (c)

Chapter 8 Numbers from Twenty-one to Fifty

1. (ii) 39 (iii) 35 (iv) 48
(vi) 48

2. (ii) 30 (iii) 31 (iv) 39 (v) 45
(vi) 48

3. (ii) 43 (iii) 48 (iv) 45 (v) 44

4. (i) False (ii) True
(iii) False (iv) True
(v) False

Chapter 9 Data Handling

1. (i) 4 (ii) 3 (ii) 2 (iv) 5
(v) 4 (vi) 3

2. (i) False (ii) True (iii) True

3. (i) (b) 7 (c) 5 (d) 6 (e) 7
(f) 8
(ii) 2 (iii) 1 (iv) 2 (v) 5
(vi) 5 (vii) 2

Chapter 10 Patterns

1. (i) P ꟼ P (ii) □ □ △
   (iii) ⟻ ⟼ ⟻
   (iv) 6 ∂ 6 (v) ↧ ⊥ ↧

4. (i) 6, 10 (ii) 30, 50, 60
   (iii) 24 (iv) 21, 20

6. (i) (b) (ii) (b) (iii) (c) (iv) (c)

Chapter 11 Numbers

2. (ii) 63 (iii) 56 (iv) 58 (v) 67

3. (ii) 52 (iii) 54 (iv) 67 (v) 69

4. (ii) 7, 6 (iii) 5, 1 (iv) 8, 2 (v) 9, 6
   (vi) 5, 9 (vii) 6, 5 (viii) 8, 4 (ix) 7, 5
   (x) 6, 6

5. (i) 78, 79, 81 (ii) 63, 64, 66
   (iii) 53, 55, 56, 58 (iv) 20, 22, 24
   (v) 71 (vi) 59
   (vii) 100

Chapter 12 Money

1. (ii)–(f), (iii)–(a), (iv)–(c),
   (v)–(b), (vi)–(d)

3. (ii) ₹ 18 (iii) ₹ 16 (iv) ₹ 12

4. (i) ✗ (ii) ✓ (iii) ✗ (iv) ✓
   (v) ✓

5. (ii)–(e), (iii)–(a),
   (iv)–(b),
   (v)–(d)

Chapter 13 How Many

1. (i) 7 (ii) 15 (iii) 18 (iv) 33
   (v) 68 (vi) 85

2. (i) ₹ 15 (ii) ₹ 8 (iii) ₹ 30 (iv) ₹ 8

3. (i) Sixteen (ii) Twenty three
   (iii) Nineteen (iv) Twenty nine
   (v) Thirty six
   (vi) Thirty one

4. (ii) 4, 6 (iii) 7, 5 (iv) 2, 4
   (v) 3, 9 (vi) 6, 2 (vii) 8, 1
   (viii) 9, 6 (ix) 4, 3 (x) 5, 1

9 789311 12209

Printed by Libri Plureos GmbH in Hamburg,
Germany